SKY WARRIORS

Also by Chris Bennett and
published by Andre Deutsch
Red Arrows: A Year in the Life
(with Tony Cunnane)

SKY WARRIORS

The Spirit of Fast Jet Flight

Chris Bennett

ANDRE
DEUTSCH

First published in Great Britain in 1997 by Andre Deutsch,
106 Great russell Street, London WC1B 3LJ
www.vci.co.uk

Andre Deutsch is a subsidiary of VCI plc

Cover and book designed by Design 23, London

British Library Cataloguing in Publication Data
A catalogue record for this title is available from the British Library

ISBN 0 233 99120 4

'High Flight' by John Magee is reproduced by permission from *This England* Magazine

Printed in Italy by Vincenzo Bona srl, Turin

Technical details of equipment used
All images reproduced in this volume were shot exclusively with Nikon F4S, F90X and F801 cameras, fitted with Nikkor lenses ranging from 16 to 400mm, and on Kodak and Fuji film stocks.
Processing by Sky Photographic, London.

For Captain Rick Lloyd, Canadian Armed Forces

Oh! I have slipped the surly bonds of Earth
And danced the skies on laughter-silvered wings;
Sunward I've climbed, and joined the tumbling mirth
Of sun-split clouds – and done a hundred things
You have not dreamed of – wheeled and soared and swung
High in the sunlit silence. Hov'ring there.
I've chased the shouting wind along, and flung
My eager craft through footless halls of air.
Up, up the long, delirious, burning blue
I've topped the wind-swept heights with easy grace
Where never lark, or even eagle flew.
And while with silent, lifting mind I've trod
The high untrespassed sanctity of space,
Put out my hand and touched the face of God.

'High Flight', John Magee

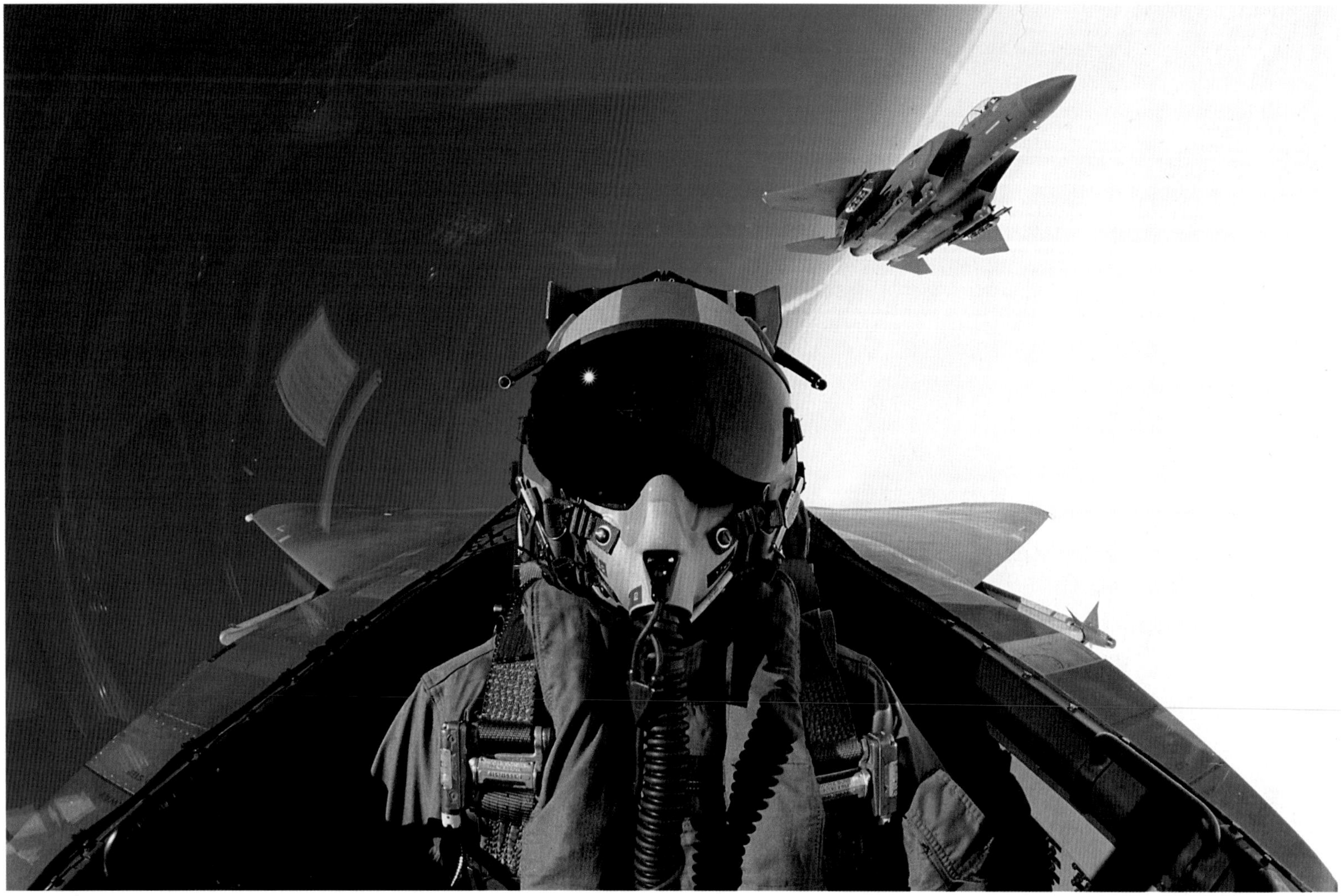

Introduction

In the world of aviation there are few aircraft as dynamic as those operated by the military – and in the world of military aviation there are few aircraft that capture the imagination so profoundly as the fast-jet. Whether used as a dedicated air-superiority fighter or as a ground-pounding bomber, the fast-jet and the people who operate them are still the elite.

Ever since the First World War, the mystique surrounding fighter aircraft and the dashing, often envied, heroes who fly them has only grown. The aircraft themselves have, of course, progressed dramatically since those early, pioneering days.

Advances in technology have brought about an extraordinary revolution in modern fighter aircraft and the often equally sleek and svelte bombers. But throughout this revolution one thing has never – will never – change: the fighter mystique lives on.

SKY WARRIORS is a personal tribute to the world of military fast-jet aviation and to those often larger-than-life characters who fly and maintain the aircraft. This volume is not intended to be an exhaustive encyclopaedia of aviation, but rather a collection of unique imagery - sometimes moving, sometimes evocative, always dynamic and exciting - which attempts to capture the true spirit of fast-jet flight.

High above the silken cumulus, a pair of Royal Air Force No 27 Squadron Tornado GR1 jets make the most of a beautiful evening. Beneath the solid overcast the ambient light would be considerably darker, the weather rather less inviting. The Tornado GR1 first entered service with the RAF in 1980, the result of a multi-national collaborative effort involving the United Kingdom, West Germany and Italy. The concept was to produce a new Multi-Role Combat Aircraft, an aircraft that, with only relatively minor differences in build, could perform both the ground attack or strike and air defence roles with equal capability.

Parked outside its HAS (Hardened Aircraft Shelter) at RAF Marham, Norfolk, England, a team of ground crew prepare the weapons fit for a Tornado GR1. Once the weapons racks are secured in place, the inert 1,000lb bombs (left) will be loaded beneath the belly of the jet. The angled slabs protruding from the rear flanks of the Tornado are the air-brakes, while the air-to-air refuelling probe extends from the right-hand-side of the jet's nose.

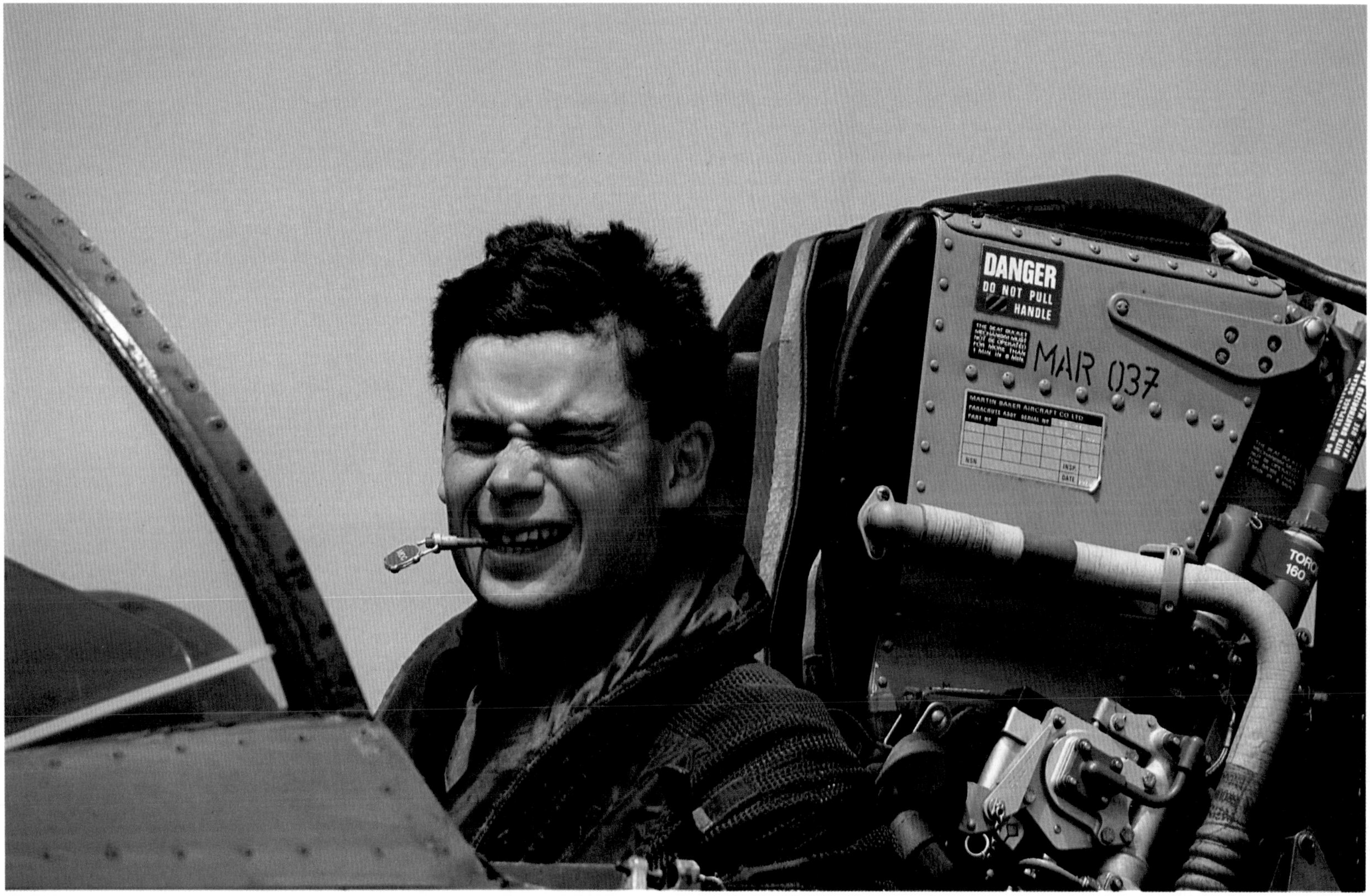

A Marham-based Tornado pilot finds his teeth a useful – albeit temporary – receptacle for one of the red-tabbed MDC safety pins. The pin is used to prevent accidental firing on the ground of the explosive Miniature Detonating Cord (MDC), which runs through the centre of the Tornado's canopy. Should the pilot have to utilise his ejection seat, the MDC would explode instantly, shattering the canopy top, through which void – fractions of a second later – both seat and pilot would be propelled.

A trio of No 2 Squadron GR1A Tornados taxi en route to the Marham runway. The GR1A is a dedicated reconnaissance variant, which uses infra-red systems to relay real-time imagery of target areas back to control.

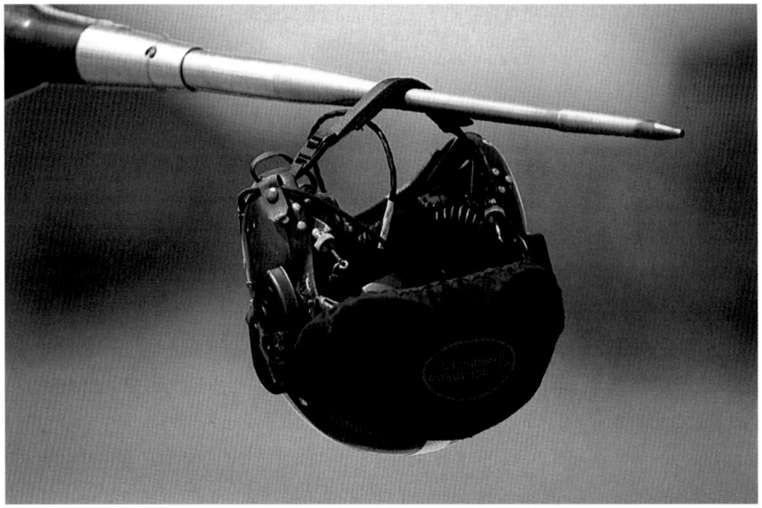

The embroidered visor cover on this flight helmet – or 'bone dome', as they are frequently called – proudly proclaims that the item of kit belongs to a member of the famous No 617 Dambuster Squadron.

With gear retracting and matching pair of Turbo-Union engines in full afterburner, this No 617 Squadron Tornado blasts off over rural Norfolk, leaving a crescendo of noise and superheated air in its wake.

The green paint adorning the thick steel casings of these 1,000lb bombs denote that they're the real thing. Inert practice versions would be painted blue.

THE NAVIGATOR'S EYE-VIEW FROM THE BACK SEAT OF A TORNADO GR1 AS IT FORMATES ON SISTER 27 SQUADRON JET. ALTHOUGH NOT AS SALUBRIOUS AS SOME OF THE STATE-OF-THE-ART AMERICAN FAST-JETS, THE ROOMY COCKPIT AND SEMI-BUBBLE CANOPY PROVIDE A COMFORTABLE WORKPLACE AND EXCELLENT LOOKOUT.

The Tornado employs a crew of two – the pilot and his navigator, who also commands the jet's weapons systems. The GR1 really proved its worth during the Gulf War, with video footage of the heroic crews, flying at the speed of sound mere feet away from the sand dunes during Operation Desert Storm, being one of the most remarkable visions of the war. The tiny blue practice bombs clasped in the weapons racks beneath the belly of the banking jet are designed to mimic the trajectory of the full-sized version, but at a fraction of the cost. A small explosive charge in the nose provides smoke evidence of the bomb's impact point.

REAR SEAT
FRONT SEAT
DANGER
ALIGN L/E OF AIR
DUCT GUARD HERE
DANGER

A prized and rare possession, the Phantom 4,000 Hours patch. This one belongs to Phil Williamson.

Another, earlier generation, two seat fighter, the McDonnell Douglas F-4 Phantom, is perhaps the most famous of all fighters. First flown in 1958, the Phantom has seen exhaustive front-line service, primarily with United States Air Force, Navy and Marine squadrons, but also with many other nations, including the Royal Air Force. At RAF Wattisham in 1991, ex-Red Arrows pilot Squadron Leader Dom Riley methodically performs his pre-start-up checks, while in the back seat (or 'pit' as it was rather accurately described) his navigator ensures that the temperamental old systems are all functioning as advertised.

The ground crew look on as the pilot and navigator of an RAF Phantom FGR2 find an external fuel tank a convenient location to complete the required paperwork. Operated by No 74 'Tiger' Squadron from Wattisham in the dedicated air-defence role, the ageing Phantom was finally struck off service in 1992, 74 Tigers being the last squadron in the RAF to fly the jet operationally.

A No 74 Squadron Phantom leaves a blanket of hot exhaust in its wake as it thunders down the runway. An F-4 in full burner is an awesome sight and sound to behold, particularly when viewed from such close quarters. The jet's twin General Electric J79 engines combine to produce a maximum thrust of 36,000lbs, capable of propelling the Phantom at speeds of mach 2.25 (1,485mph) at 40,000 feet, and up to an operational altitude of 62,000 feet.

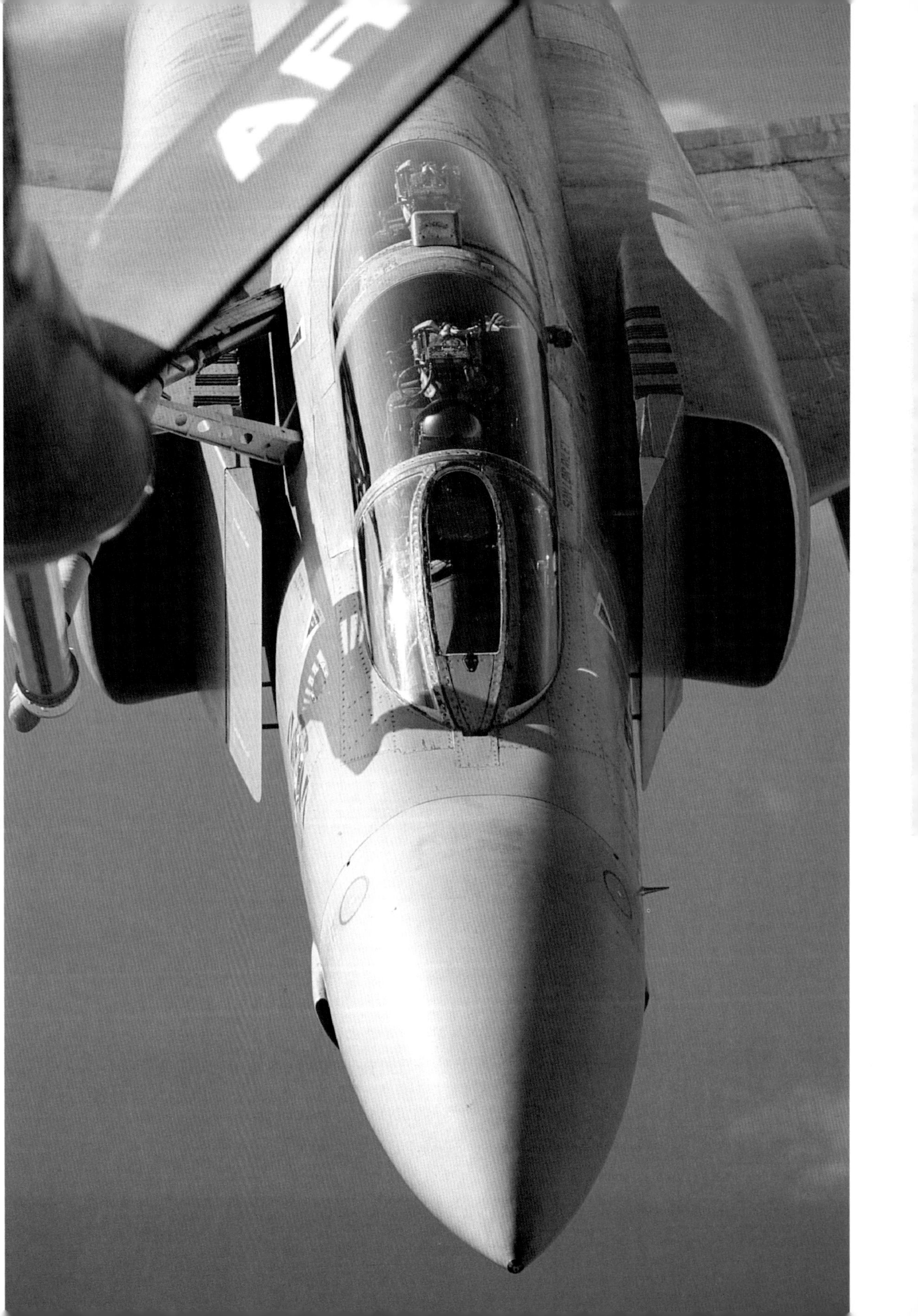

Holding station to the rear of a KC-135 tanker, this 74 Squadron Phantom tops up its fuel load, the jet's air refuelling probe mated to the tanker's basket, the union visible through the shadow cast upon the F-4's nose.

Wing Commander Graham Clark, Officer Commanding No 74 Squadron, cruises at altitude high in the deep blue yonder as the camera ship F-4 formates in May 1991. This was a memorable day for me. Although deeply privileged to have flown in the back seat of an F-4, the restricted forward visibility, combined with high cockpit sills and an imperfect canopy, became a recipe for air sickness. It was also a memorable day for Flight-Lieutenant Tony Dixon, Wing Commander Clark's navigator – his last flight in the Phantom before leaving No 74 Squadron. Tony now has a part-time job with the Battle of Britain Memorial Flight, acting as navigator in the Lancaster and Dakota.

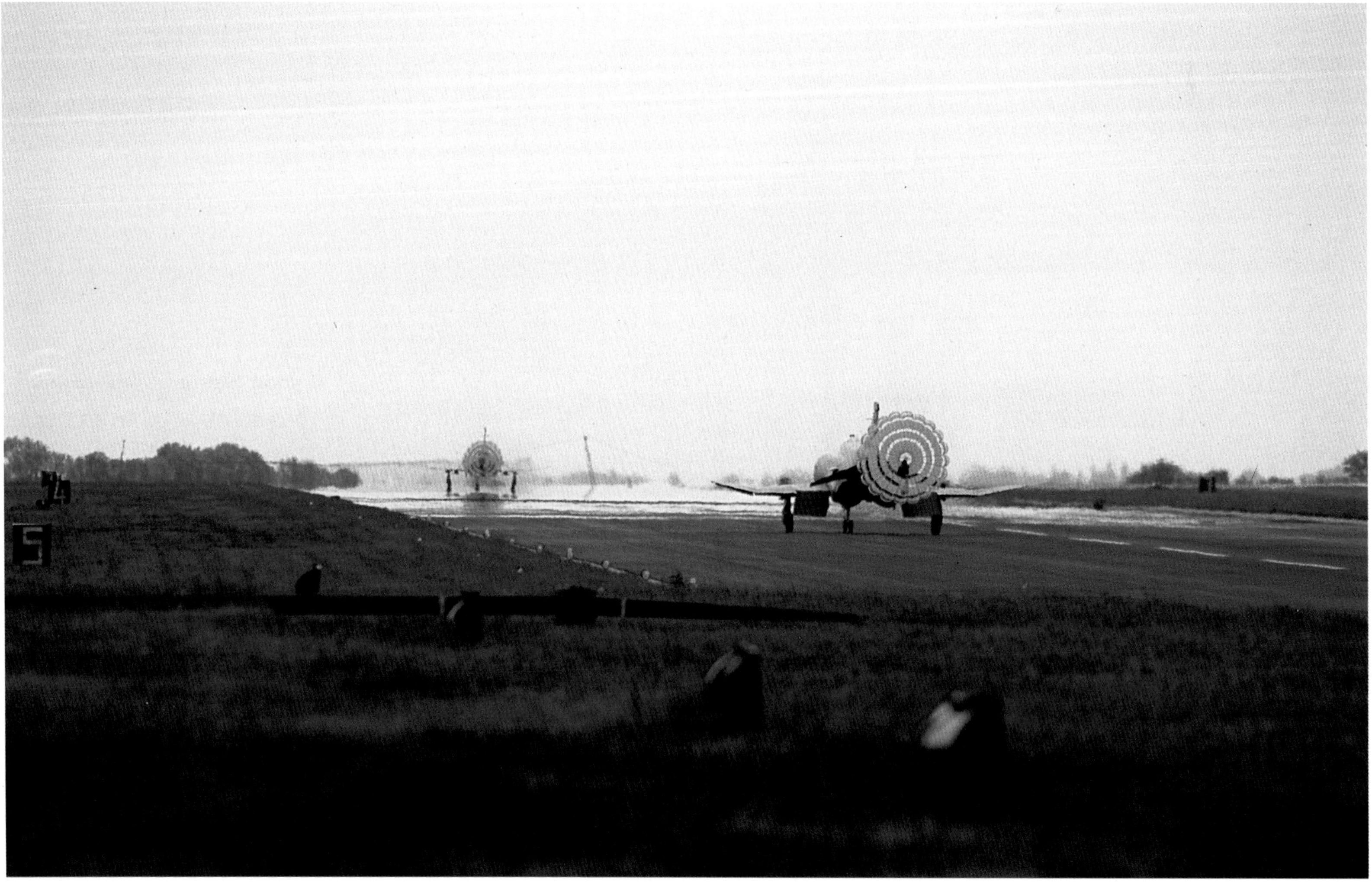

In the Phantom's twilight hours, a pair of jets take the runway at Wattisham, drogue parachutes deployed to more rapidly decelerate their forward velocity. Soon the Phantom would be no more – the majority sold for scrap – being cut up in a most undignified manner, just the lucky few escaping to become static, lifeless exhibits at museums, or 'gate guardians' at RAF stations. Once stripped of their beloved Phantoms, 74 Squadron was disbanded on 1 October 1992, re-forming one year later at RAF Valley in Wales as a reserve squadron flying Hawk trainers.

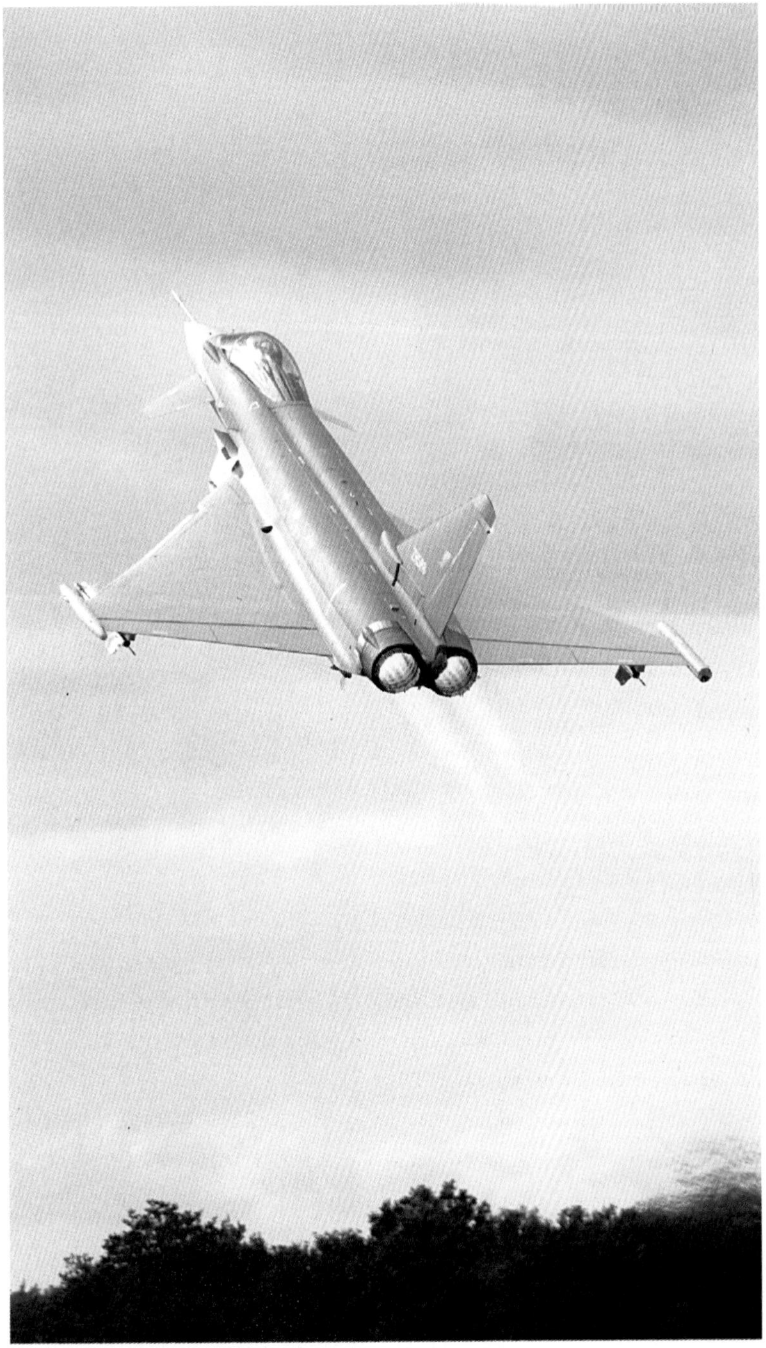

From yesteryear's combat-proven technology to the as yet unproven technology of tomorrow. The multi-national Eurofighter 2000 takes to the air at Farnborough '96 to demonstrate its abilities before a technology hungry audience. Due to enter service early in the new century, Eurofighter will replace the ageing Jaguar and complement the RAF's Tornado force.

THE ROYAL NAVY'S AIRCRAFT CARRIER HMS ARK ROYAL MANOEUVRES TO DROP ANCHOR OFF LISBON, PORTUGAL. A MEMBER OF THE 'INVISIBLE' CLASS OF SHIPS, THE 20,000 TON FULL LOAD DISPLACEMENT ARK ROYAL WAS COMMISSIONED INTO SERVICE IN 1985.

WITH PILOTS STRAPPED IN AND EAGER FOR ACTION, THE FLIGHT-DECK CREW AWAIT ORDERS TO COMMAND THE SPOOLING UP OF ENGINES AND REMOVAL OF RETAINING CHAINS FROM THE SEA HARRIER FRS1 JETS.

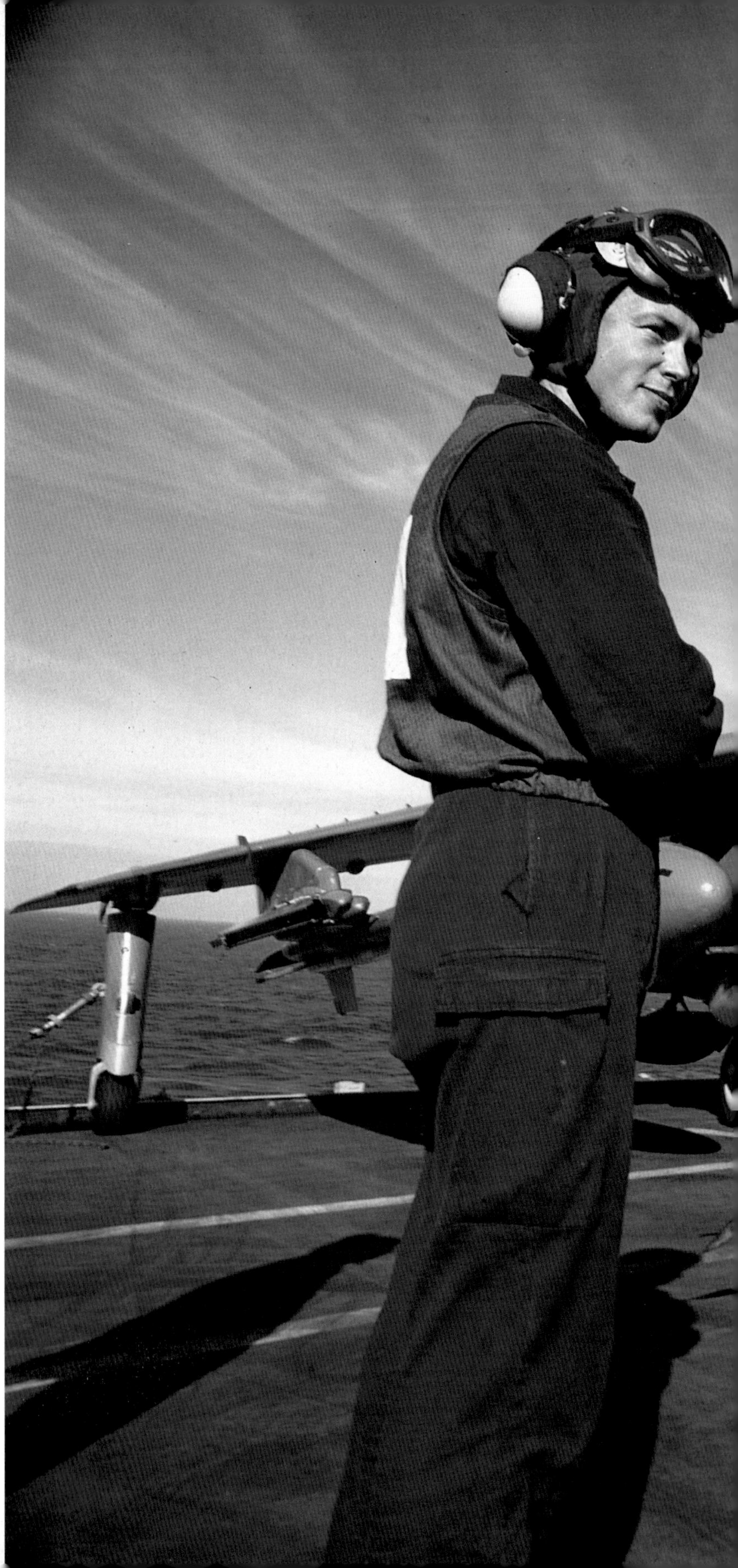

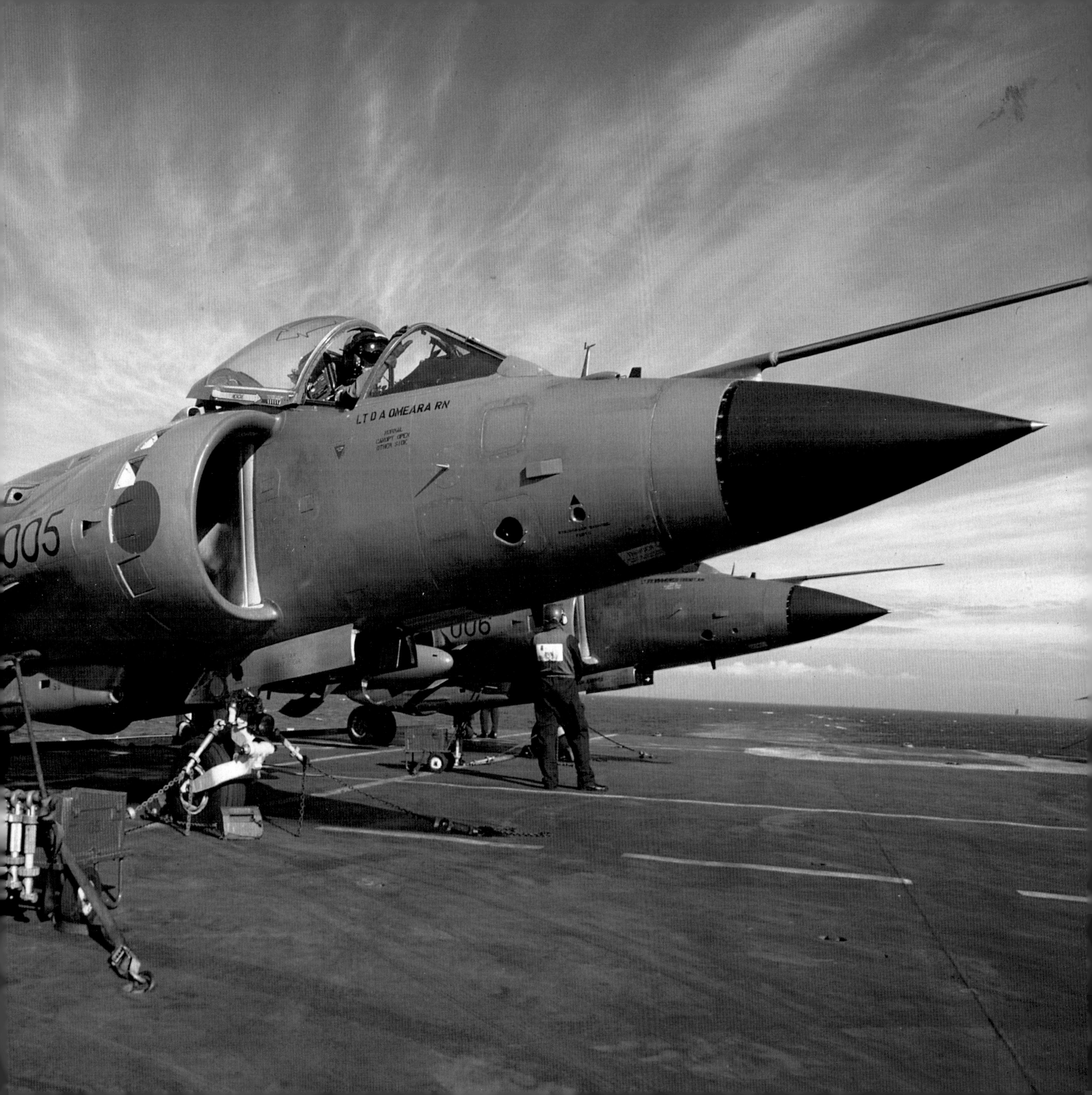
LT D A OMEARA RN
005
006

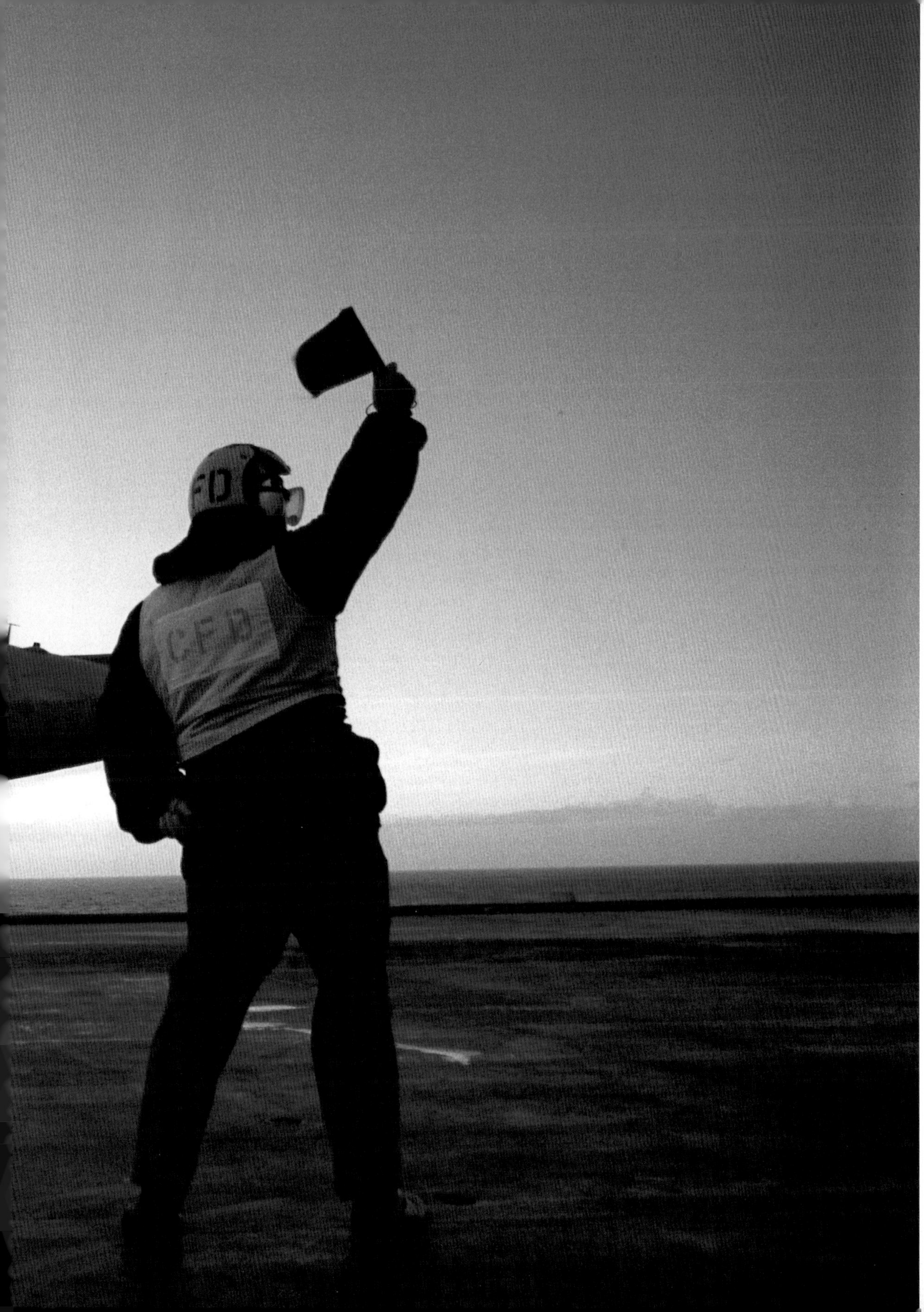

A stiff early morning breeze down the deck signifies the carrier is sailing into wind as a Sea Harrier throttles up to maximum power in anticipation of being flagged off the ARK ROYAL's flight-deck.

A Sea Harrier takes to the air, using the ramped 'ski jump' for the purpose. The vertical and short take off and landing (VSTOL) Harrier has permitted shorter flight-decks and eliminated the need for expensive catapult and arrestor gear seen on United States Navy carriers. The elevated ramp enables jets to launch with greater payloads than would otherwise be possible.

As the sun descends below the yardarm, one of the ARK's flight-deck crew ventures out to check his aircraft. The tranquil scene belies the noise, activity and danger that will erupt once the night flying programme gets underway.

Designed for strike and close air support of ground forces, but with a dog-fighting capability, the Harrier has been a success story for British Aerospace and will continue to see front line service for many years to come.

The sleek, streamlined nose of an F-16 Fighting Falcon takes on a sinister guise as it protrudes from within the darkened recesses of a hardened shelter at Bodø, in northern Norway.

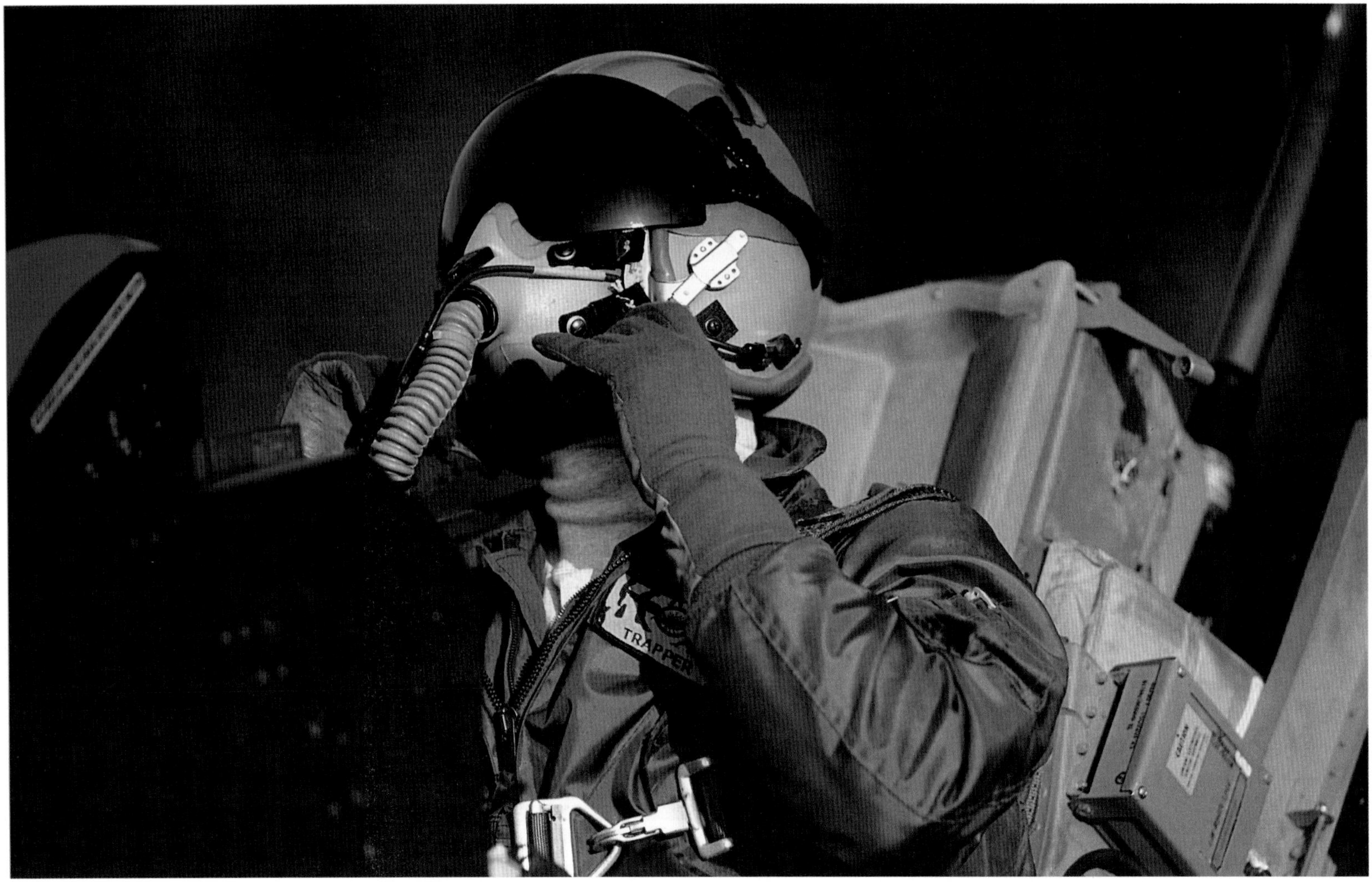

A visitor to the Canadian Armed Forces base at Baden Söllingen, this Dutch F-16 pilot checks his American manufactured flight kit prior to firing up the Falcon's Pratt and Whitney F100 engine. Although the General Dynamics designed and built F-16 has been in service for nearly two decades, it is still one of the hottest jets around. A true multi-role fighter, the lightweight 'Viper' is equally at ease in close air support and strike roles or in air superiority dogfighting.

Having successfully sorted out his kit, Trapper taxis the F-16B off into the sunset. The 'B' model is a tandem two-seat version of the more common standard single seat jet, characterized by the rather elongated appearance of this F-16's canopy. The Fighting Falcon is fully 'fly-by-wire', meaning that when the pilot initiates a manoeuvre with his control column (or, in the case of the F-16, his side-stick), rather than moving physical cables, he actually sends electronic impulses to the jet's on-board computer, which then commands the relevant control surfaces to activate appropriately.

The pilot of this Dutch F-16 reefs his jet energetically into a very steep climb-out, the blast cone of hot air instantly vapourizing moisture in its wake on the wet Leeuwarden runway.

WITH UNDERCARRIAGE SELECTED AND AIR BRAKES DEPLOYED, A ROYAL NETHERLANDS AIR FORCE 323 SQUADRON F-16 IS BRACED FOR TOUCHDOWN. ONE OF TWO F-16 SQUADRONS BASED AT LEEUWARDEN IN HOLLAND, 323 'DIANA' SQUADRON HAS BEEN OPERATING THE JET – PRINCIPALLY IN THE AIR-DEFENCE ROLE – SINCE 1986.

With dark visor selected against the bright sun at Mildenhall '97, Flight-Lieutenant Sean Perrett – alias 'Red Nine' - is strapped in and ready to roll. Standing proudly on the cockpit combing is Sean's newly acquired mascot, the famous Walt Disney TOY STORY character, Buzz Lightyear, who will accompany Sean on every display in the 1997 season.

Flight-Lieutenant Andy 'Cubes' Cubin, MBE, fastens his Mae West before stepping into the front office of a Red Arrows' Hawk. The Red Arrows, or, more formally, the RAF Aerobatic Team (RAFAT), have been thrilling audiences around the world with their precision formation flying since 1965. Originally, the team used Folland Gnats, converting to the then new British Aerospace Hawk (the current RAF advanced jet trainer) in 1979.

The magnificent Red Arrows loop in 'Feathered Arrow' formation over RAF Akrotiri, Cyprus, during one of the many pre-season training flights undertaken to perfect their display. The art of safe, precision formation aerobatics requires the utmost in skill and practice each year. Once the early winter training has been completed, the Team transits to Akrotiri for 'Springhawk', taking advantage of the favourable weather there to put the final polish on the season's display.

Red Arrows' pilots are selected from the very best in the RAF, usually highly experienced, in their late-twenties and early-thirties, with perhaps 2,000 hours flying fast jets. They need this level of experience: the flying demands it.

During early training, the formation may be split into odd groups, hence this asymmetrical arrow looping in the deep blue wintry skies over RAF Cranwell, the Red Arrows' home base in Lincolnshire.

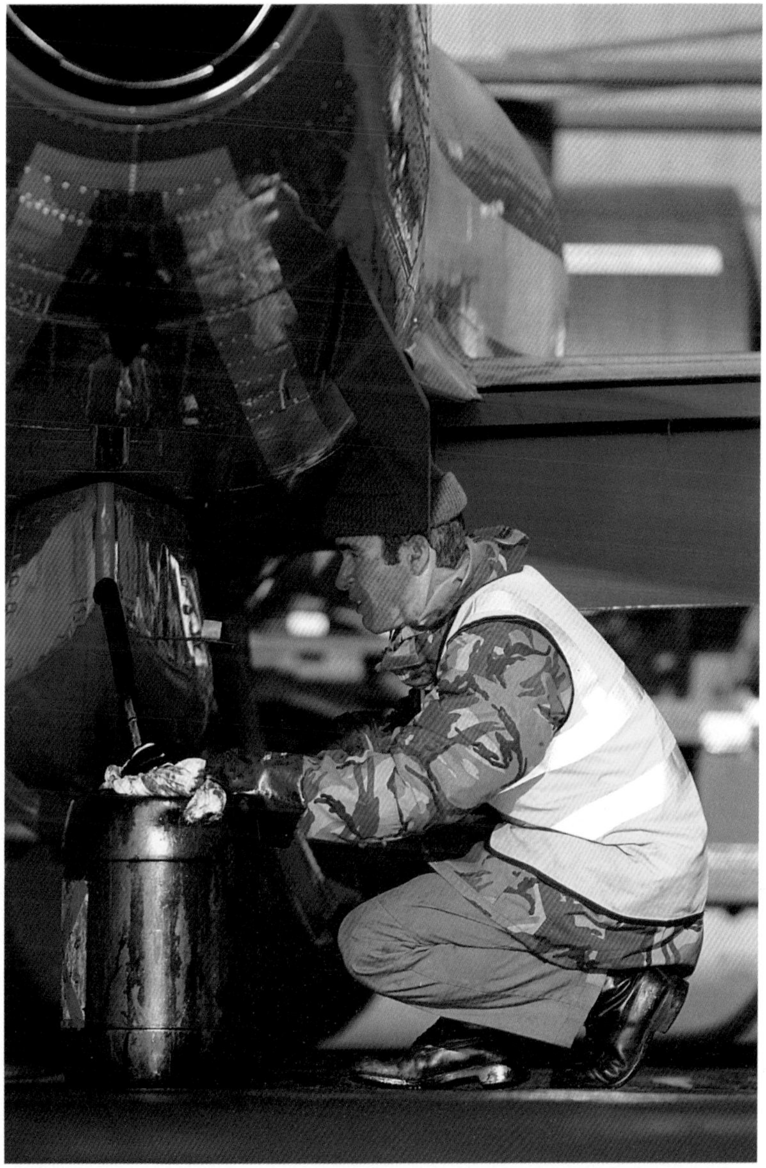

One of the dirtiest but nevertheless essential jobs on the Team is the refilling of the smoke system with diesel and dye after every sortie. The white smoke is created by injecting diesel into the jet efflux and the colours red and blue by adding the relevant dye.

An orderly parade of Jaguar GR1s await their pilots on a misty morning at RAF Coltishall. Unlike most modern fighter bases, Coltishall has no hardened shelters and therefore the jets are either left outside or hangared.

The sun rises and is starting to burn off the mist as the ground crews prepare their aircraft for the day's hectic flight schedule. The Jaguar, unusually, has the facility to carry Sidewinder heat-seeking missiles for self defence on over-wing rails, the finless example on the port side rail in this case being a purely inert captive training version.

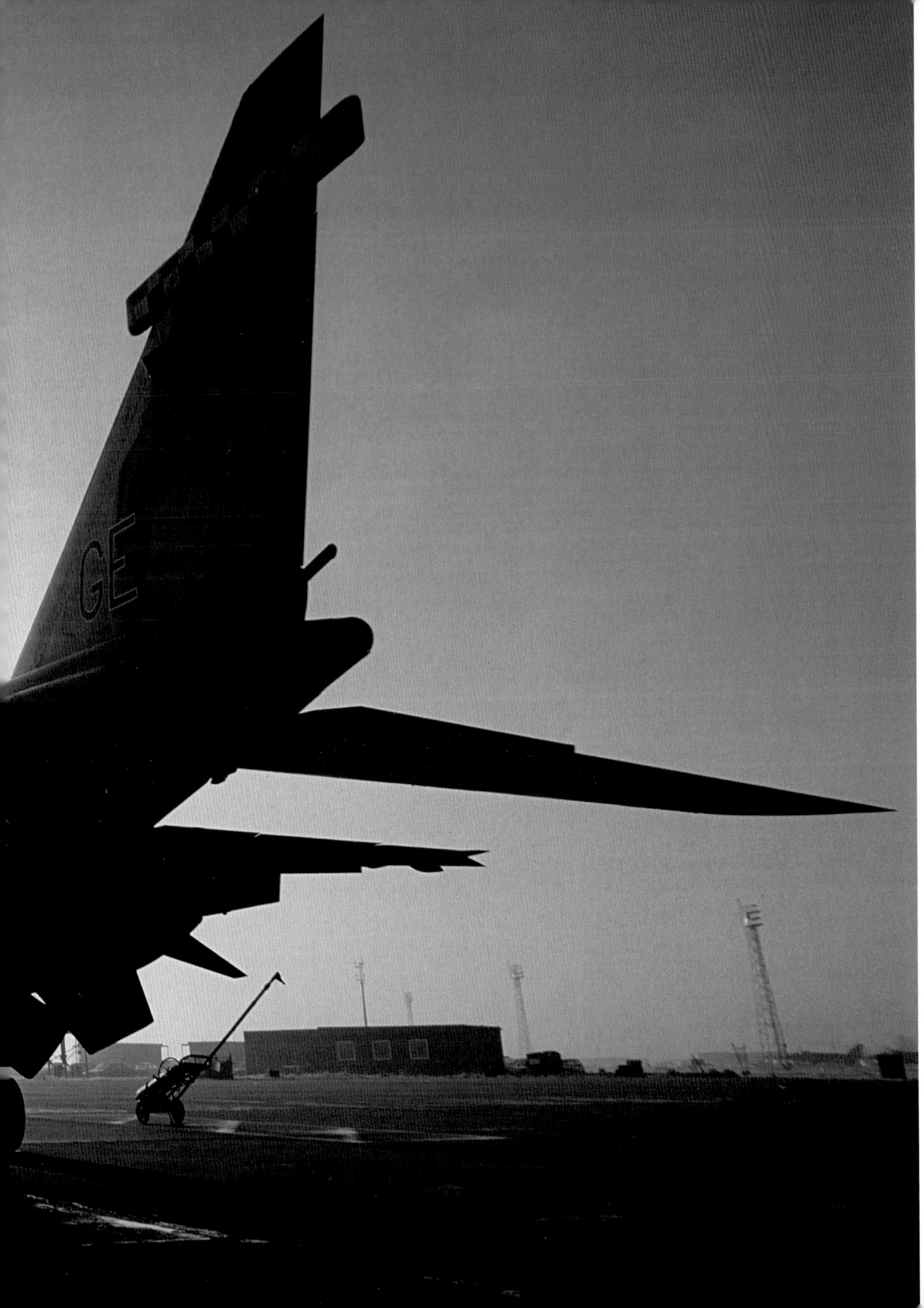

Before climbing into the cockpit, the pilot performs a methodical pre-flight walk round, looking for any possible snags with the jet. The blue and yellow chequers on the tail fin tip identify this Jaguar as belonging to No 54 Squadron, a Coltishall resident since 1974. The 'Colt' Jaguars performed admirably during the Gulf War in the close air support of ground forces and reconnaissance roles.

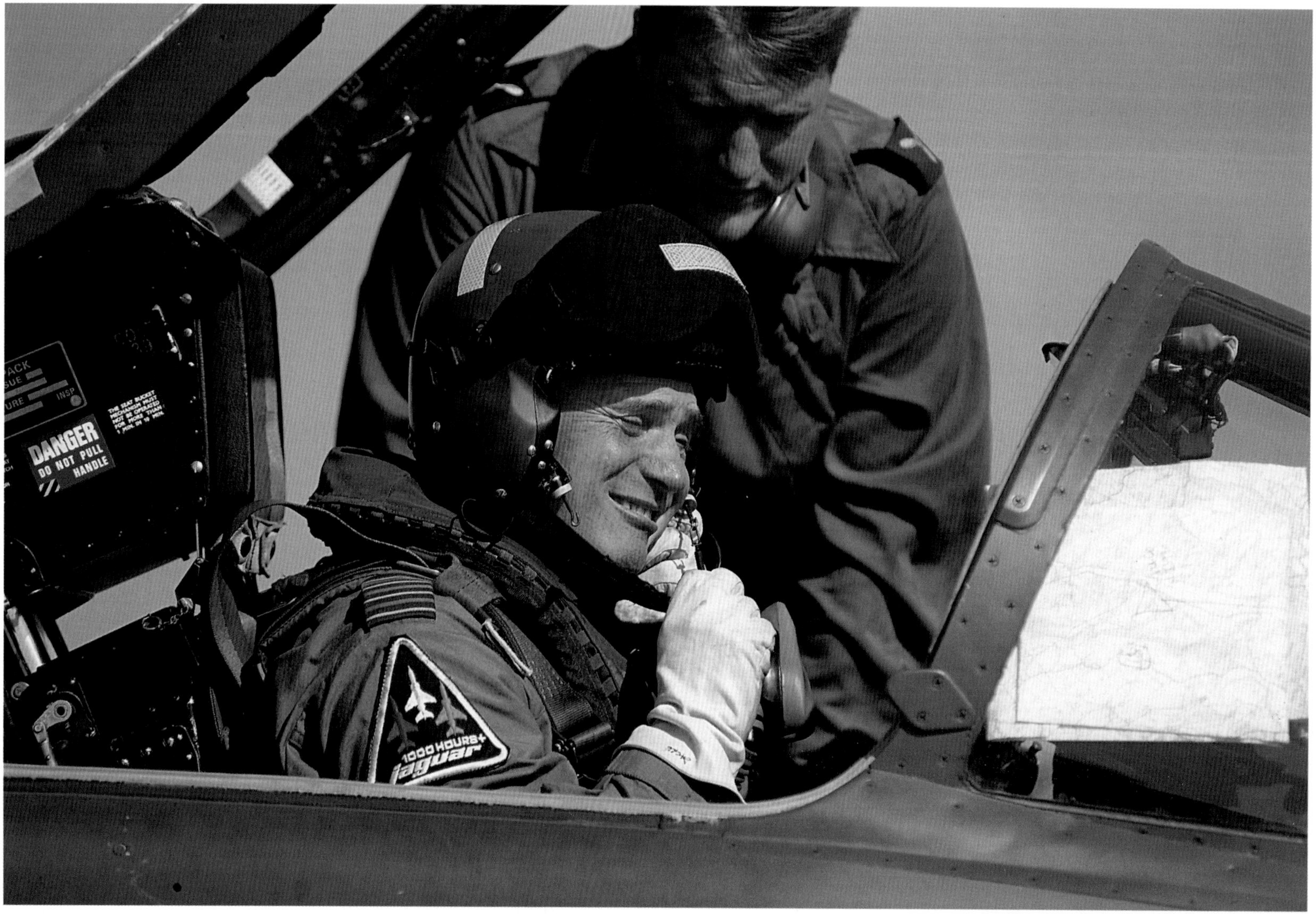

Group Captain Phil Dacre, Station Commander of RAF Coltishall in 1992, tackles the always fiddly business of fastening chin strap and oxygen mask. Although his primary task was to run RAF Coltishall and to look after the people who served there, Group Captain Dacre always liked to keep his hand in, flying a Jaguar with one of Colt's three resident squadrons whenever possible.

With flaps and under-carriage down and landing light ablaze, a sand coloured ex-Desert Storm Jaguar is just seconds from roaring over my head to touch down on Coltishall's runway. The large, bulbous canisters hanging from the inboard wing pylons are fuel tanks, not bombs.

CUT HERE
EMERGENCY
DANGER
RESCUE

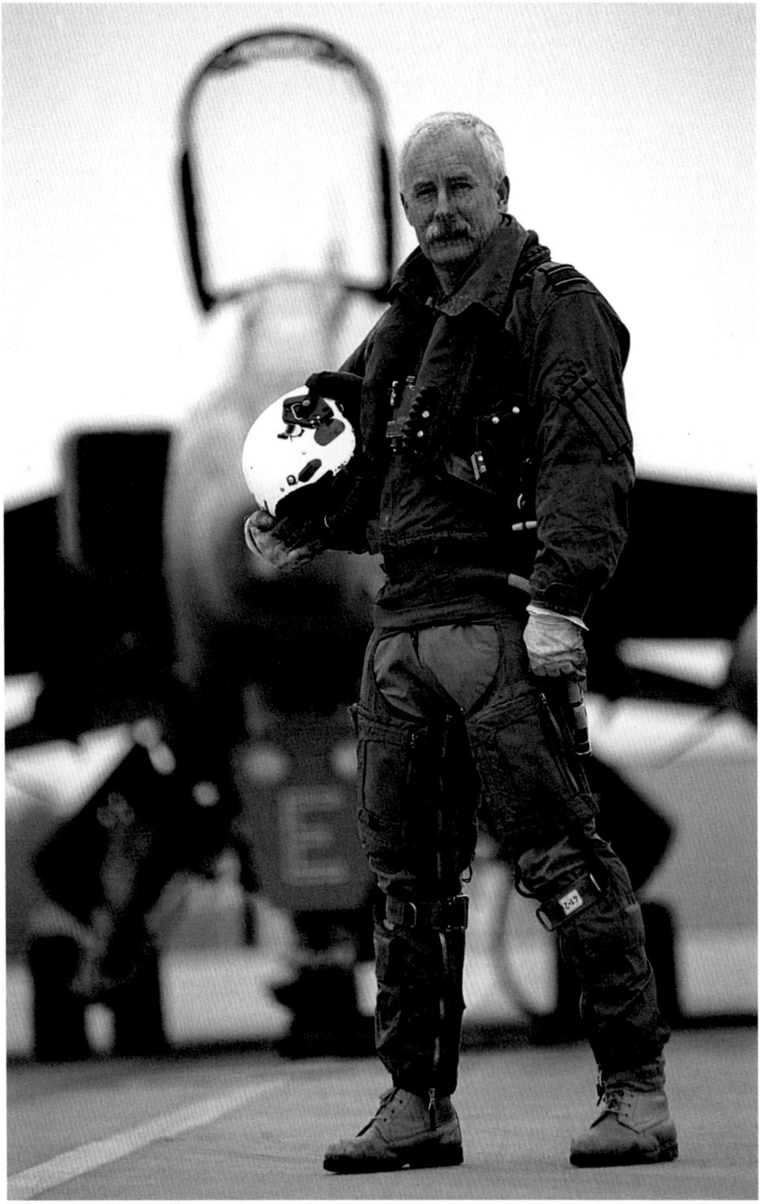

Canadian-born Squadron Leader Dave 'Baggers' Bagshaw poses for one last 'hero' shot in front of his Jaguar on 7 February 1992. Earlier that day he had flown his last operational sortie in the Jaguar before retiring, having chalked up over 4,200 hours on type, the vast majority with No 41 Squadron at Coltishall.

The twin raised canopies identify this Jaguar as being a T2A conversion trainer, virtually identical to the normal single seat GR1A version, but generally used for instruction and check rides (and occasionally even for flying photographers!). The Jaguar is likely to be phased out early in the next century, its redundancy completed by the introduction of the new multi-role Eurofighter.

The steely eye glancing in the rear-view mirror belongs to Squadron Leader Mike Rondot. Now retired from the air force, Mike is well known for his dynamic and atmospheric oil paintings of jet-fighters – many of which, not unnaturally, feature the Jaguar. For an older-generation jet, the canopy of the Jaguar provides a reasonably good lookout, better than some, but not as wonderfully panoramic as the modern breed of American fighters.

The Brothers Bagshaw. 4,000 Hour veteran, Squadron Leader Dave 'Baggers' Bagshaw is joined in the air on his last operational sortie by younger brother Lieutenant Colonel John 'Baggy' Bagshaw. John, commander of the Canadian Armed Forces 421 Tactical Fighter Squadron (TFS) from Baden Söllingen in Germany, brought his CF-18 Hornet over especially for the occasion. It was the first time the two intrepid aviating brothers had met on the wing.

2

When it comes to panoramic views, the F/A-18's bubble canopy provides one of the most scenic of all, as this 'hero' shot of me in the back seat of a Canadian CF-18 testifies.

On a damp but fresh morning at Baden Söllingen, a pair of CF-18 Hornets complete their take-off runs, vortices spiralling liberally off the jets' wing tips as moisture is squeezed from the water laden air. Birds are a constant menace at bases operating jet-powered aircraft. The two seen flying across the picture could so easily have been sucked into a jet's air intake, the result almost certainly proving terminal for the multi-million dollar engine. It probably wouldn't do the bird much good either.

A Canadian Armed Forces operated Hornet from Söllingen banks over the multi-coloured fields of the Black Forest area of Germany. The blue tube on the F-18's starboard wing tip rail is a Captive Air Training Missile (CATM), a totally inert version of the AIM-9 Sidewinder heat-seeking air-to-air missile. For this purpose, however, it does have a live infra-red seeker head, enabling the pilot to acquire and 'lock on' targets during air combat training.

439 TFS is one of the elite group of squadrons world wide that utilizes a tiger's head as its emblem. Each year these squadrons get together at the annual 'Tiger Meet', often painting a jet in spectacular tiger stripes for the event. 439 Squadron's 1992 example was masterfully understated, the subtle two-tone grey still enabling the Hornet to be used for operational training. The more common yellow and black paint schemes don't really promote stealthy, low-visibility in the airborne arena!

(Far left) Lieutenant-Colonel John 'Baggy' Bagshaw leads his 421 Squadron mates in a perfectly executed fan break, each jet peeling off three seconds after the last.

Two other Hornets hold off as the boss of 439 Squadron, Lieutenant-Colonel Mike Stacey, prepares to plug 'Tiger One' into a USAF C130 tanker for a top-up of motion lotion.

Once again, the superb visibility afforded by this amazing aircraft is dramatically demonstrated as, in turn, RAF exchange pilot Flight Lieutenant Dave 'Billy' Billington brings the camera ship in for a quick drink. Hope they take American Express!

Baggy takes his 421 TFS Hornet in close to give us a good look at those AIM-9 Sidewinder missiles – and at the 'spoof' canopy painted on the underside of the fuselage, designed to momentarily confuse an opponent in the midst of a heated dogfight.

Colonel Stacey slots Tiger One in on our six o'clock. In a real dogfight we'd be dead.

In full zone five afterburner, this Canadian Hornet lights the pipes and accelerates down the Söllingen runway in a spectacular fashion, intent on some obligatory night flying practice.

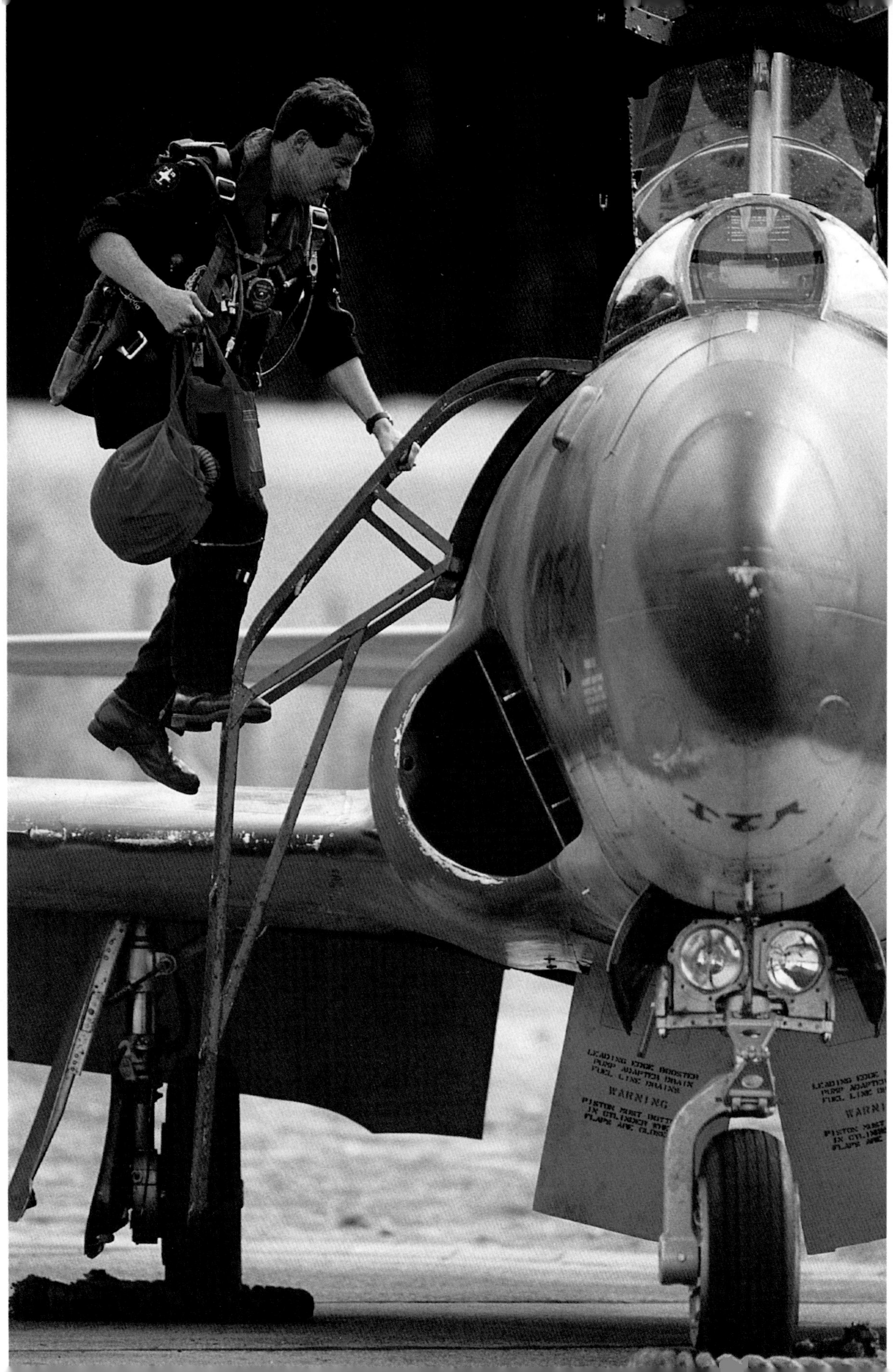

Captain Hart Proksch climbs aboard an example of one of the most successful jet trainers ever built – the Lockheed T-33 Shooting Star, commonly referred to as the T-Bird. Four of these charismatic old jets were kept at Söllingen for general liaison duty and air crew proficiency flights.

A matching pair of T-33s fly past the picturesque and typically Bavarian Hohenzollern Schloss. Powered by a single Rolls-Royce Nene turbojet, the sleek Shooting Star could push along at speeds of up to 450 knots at low level. The T-33 is responsible for training thousands of US Air Force pilots in years gone by, many of whom would have seen active service in the skies over Vietnam in the F-4 Phantom.

312

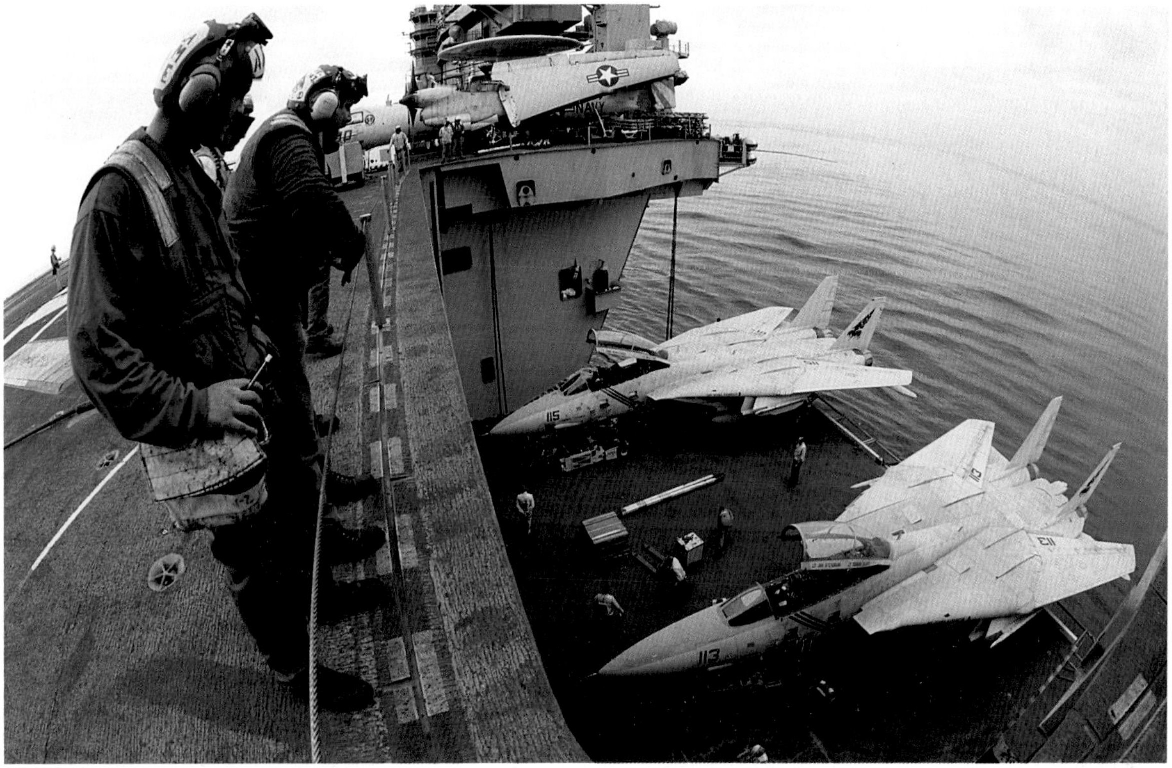

Members of the GEORGE WASHINGTON's youthful flight-deck crew look on as two F-14 Tomcats are hoisted up from the hangar deck, via elevator three, aft of the Island.

On board the USS GEORGE WASHINGTON CVN-73, one of the United States Navy's fleet of formidable 97,000 ton nuclear powered 'Super Carriers', an A-6 Intruder is just a blink of an eye from catching one of the four arresting cables that span the flight-deck for a successful 'trap'.

Aircraft carriers such as the USS George Washington regularly accommodate nearly eighty aircraft, many of which are F/A-18 Hornets and F-14 Tomcats – both dual-role fighters. When the weather is favourable, particularly on no fly days, a high percentage of the carrier's complement of jets will be found neatly parked and chained up on the flight-deck.

Having replenished a Tomcat's six-barrelled 20mm Vulcan 'Gatling' cannon, a pair of armourers exit stage right with the automatic loading device. In a combat situation, firing nearly 100 rounds per second at full speed, it wouldn't take long to exhaust the jet's 675-round capacity.

22

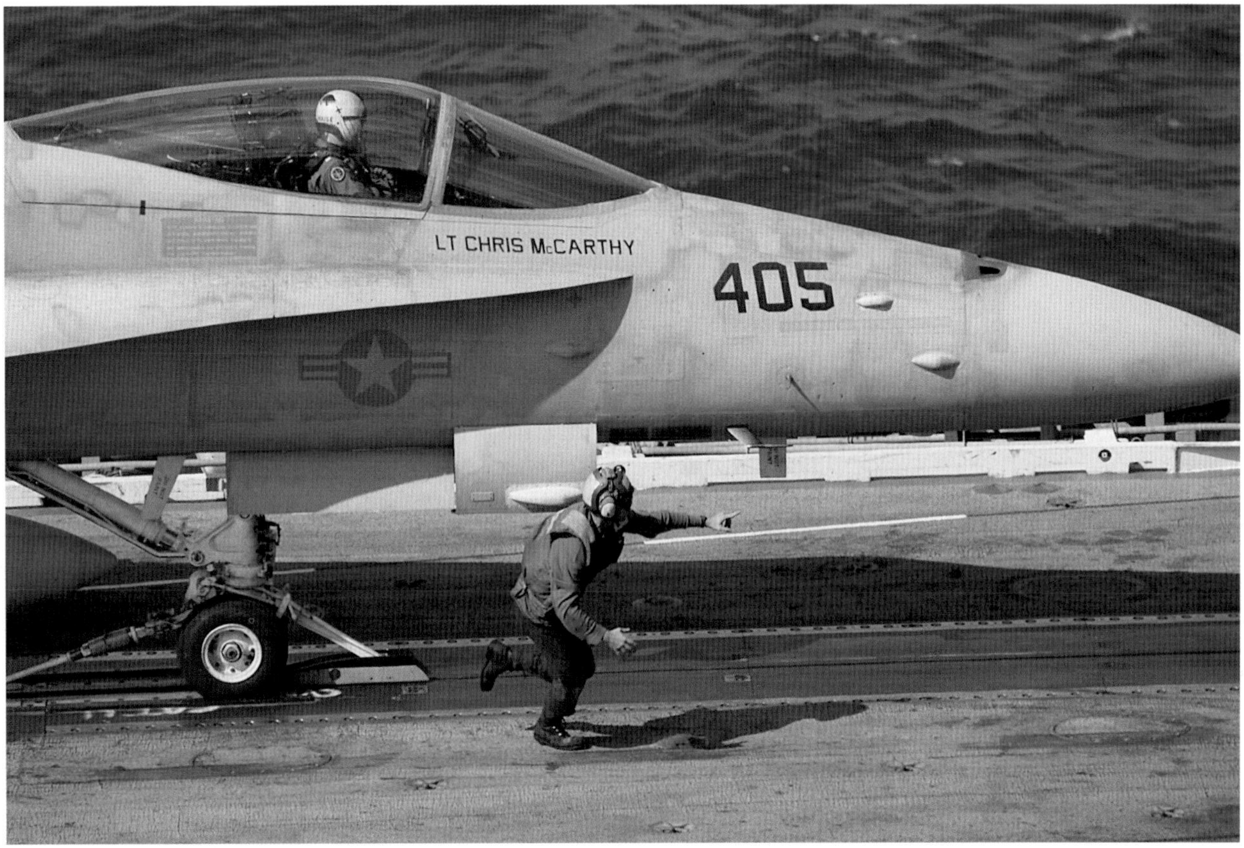

United States Navy aircraft-carriers use awesomely powerful steam catapults to almost literally fling the jets off the deck. Having successfully coupled this F/A-18 Hornet's nose tow-bar to the catapult shuttle, the hook-up man sprints clear, gesturing to the catapult officer that all is in readiness for the launch. Almost instantaneously, the catapult will hit full power, breaking the holdback connection aft of the nosewheel leg, permitting the now untethered jet to accelerate along the deck from 0 to 150 mph in just two seconds.

WILDCATS

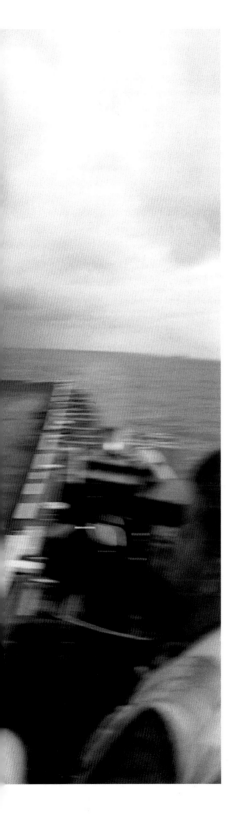

At night on the carrier some aircraft remain chained to the flight-deck while others are brought down below into the hangar. During the nocturnal hours the hangar deck takes on a surreal appearance, dimly illuminated by low-powered, orangey sodium lighting

With tailhook bringing up the rear, a VFA-131 Wildcats Hornet comes in over the USS GEORGE WASHINGTON's fantail and prepares to slam down on to the carrier's steel deck, hopefully snagging a wire in the process. In the foreground, the Landing Signals Officers (LSOs) monitor and grade the jet's approach, the accuracy of which is vital for a safe and successful trap.

The modern United States Navy Supercarrier is a floating airport of incredible potential power. With its mixed complement of aircraft and an awesome array of weaponry at its disposal, the carrier has the ability to project mobile military might anywhere in the world within reach of the sea. But, thankfully, most often this destructive potential is used as a deterrent, disuading would be aggressors from actual hostile action. The carriers traverse the world's oceans, acting as roving ambassadors for the United States and as roving international peace-keepers for the common good.

CAPT M BRANCH
300
ADC AW KEN EDWARDS
BRONX, NY.
0051

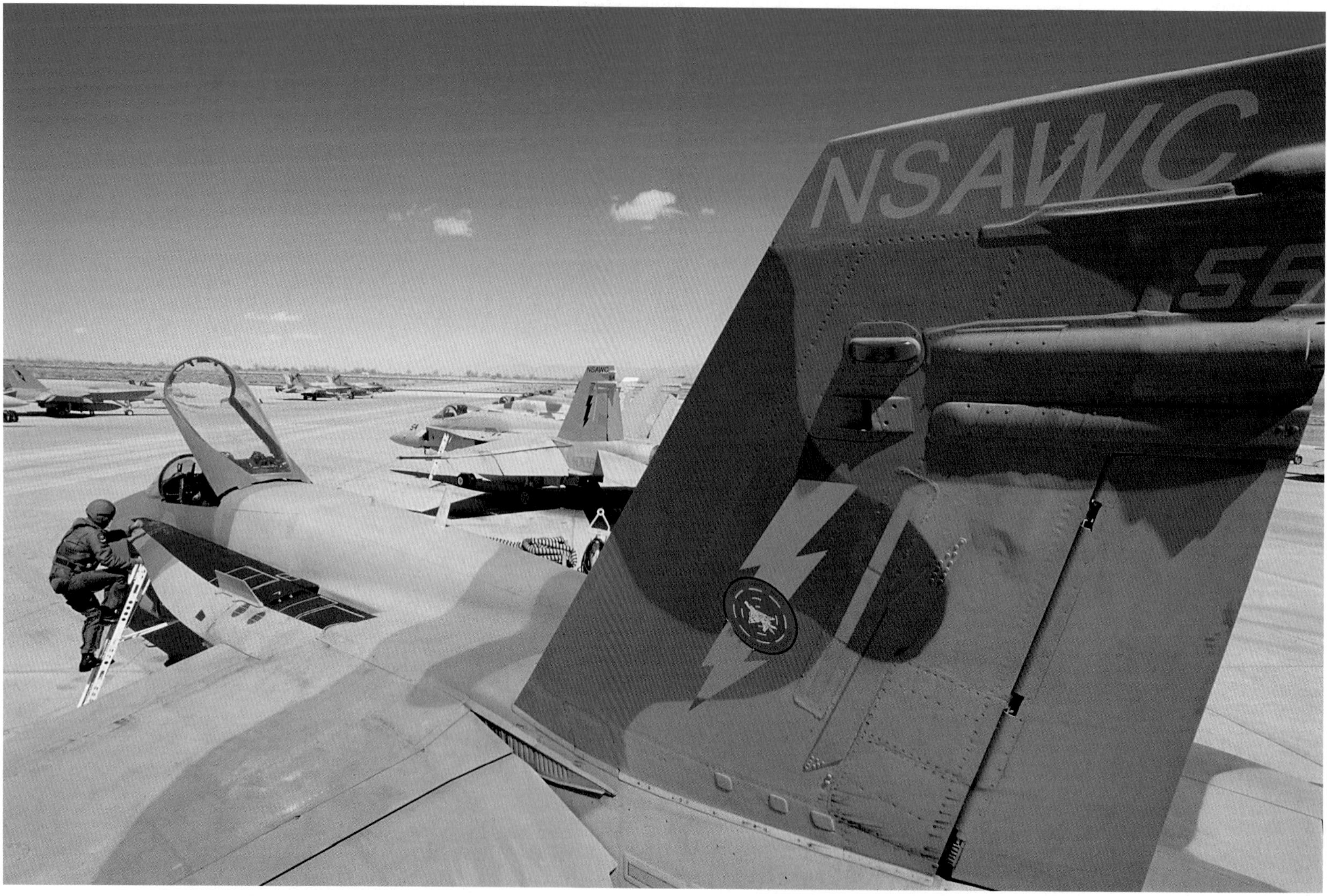

Lieutenant-Commander Michael 'Beads' Smith climbs aboard his Navy Strike and Air Warfare Centre (NSAWC) F/A-18 Hornet at NAS Fallon, situated sixty miles from Reno in the Nevada Desert. Formed in 1996, NSAWC (pronounced 'N-sock') combines the air-defence dogfighting skills of the US Navy's legendary TOPGUN Fighter Weapons School, with the bombing skills of their 'Strike University'. Although no longer recognized formally, unsurprisingly perhaps, the TOPGUN name lives on – hence the multi-coloured decal that adorns the vertical stabiliser of Beads's F/A-18.

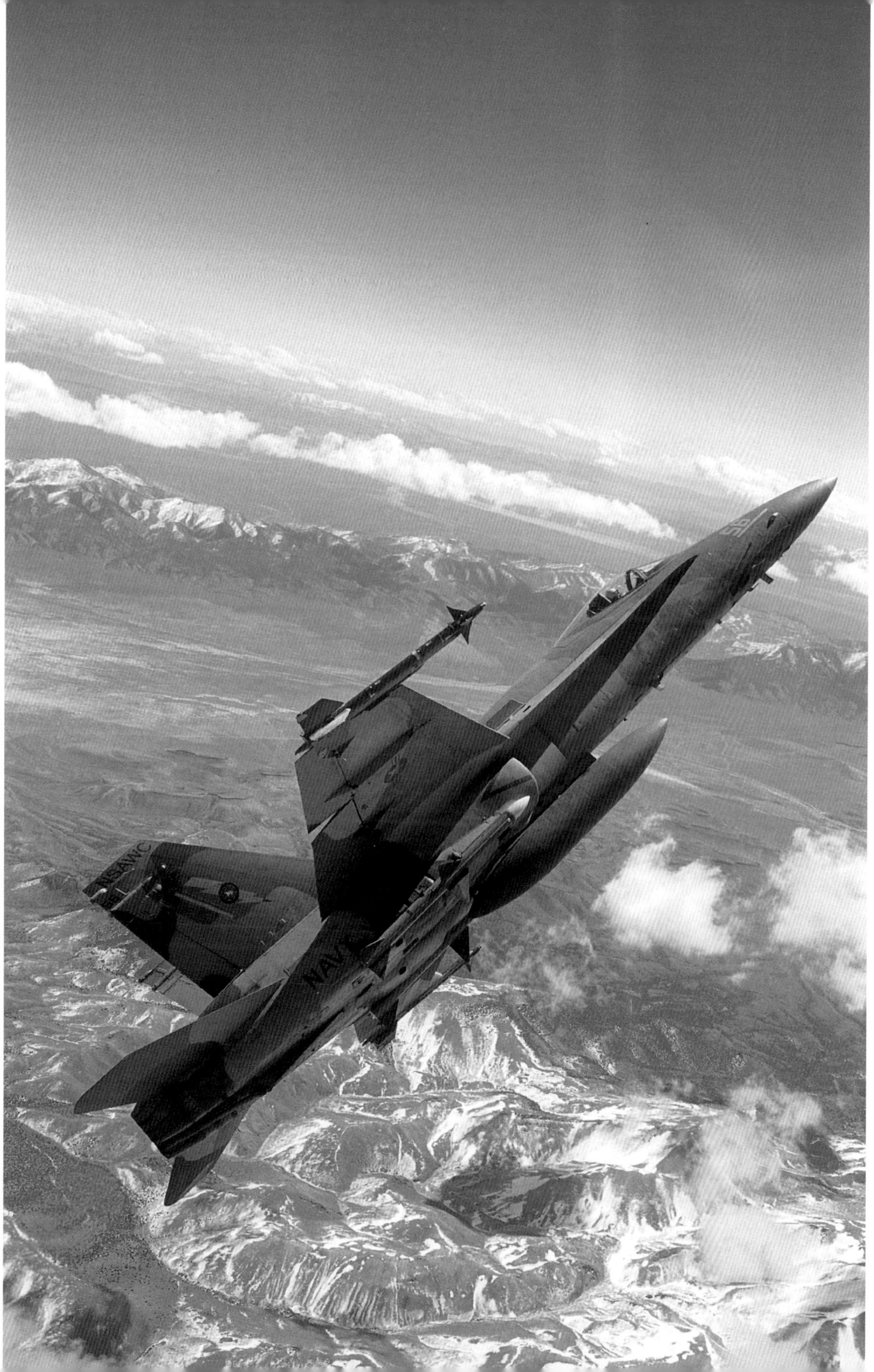

A United States Navy TOPGUN Hornet demonstrates its outstanding agility high over the snow-capped mountains of Nevada. Navy Strike and Air Warfare Centre jets are painted in adversary colours intended to simulate those of potentially hostile foreign nations. This F/A-18's paintwork is designed to represent the Iraqi Air Force's desert camouflage. TOPGUN instructor pilots, picked from the best that the Navy has to offer, fly the jets in such a way as to mimic the adversary air force's airborne techniques and doctrine, the visiting student fleet pilots learning by experience how to defend against – and defeat – such tactics.

Reefing into the pure vertical, one of the NSAWC adversary F/A-18 strike fighters pops a string of decoy flares into its wake. Made of magnesium, the flares burn at a substantially higher temperature than the jet efflux produced by the fighter's engine, the plan being to fool and confuse a heat-seeking missile into following one of the decoy flares instead of the jet's hot tail-pipe.

The TOPGUN Navy Strike and Air Warfare Centre operates two different types of jet, the F/A-18 Hornet and the F-14A Tomcat. With these, and with the highly experienced TOPGUN pilots using differing and appropriate tactics, most types and generations of adversary fighters' manoeuvres can be simulated. Painted in Russian colours and intended to represent the MiG-21, the third smaller jet in this formation is a Northrop F-5 Tiger 11 belonging to VFC-13, a Navy Aggressor Squadron also based at Fallon.

Seated high upon the Martin Baker ejection seat of a TOPGUN F-14 Tomcat, TOPGUN boss Commander Rolland 'Dawg' Thompson completes his post start-up checks. Whereas the older generation jets were designed to perform either the air defence or the strike roles, current generation fighters can perform both equally well, hence the amalgamation of TOPGUN and Strike U into one single training facility - NSAWC. The down side, for the TOPGUN instructors at least, is that it meant moving the Fighter Weapons School from its traditional west coast Californian Miramar home to the equally sunny but rather less glamorous Fallon. Tom 'Maverick' Cruise would not have approved!

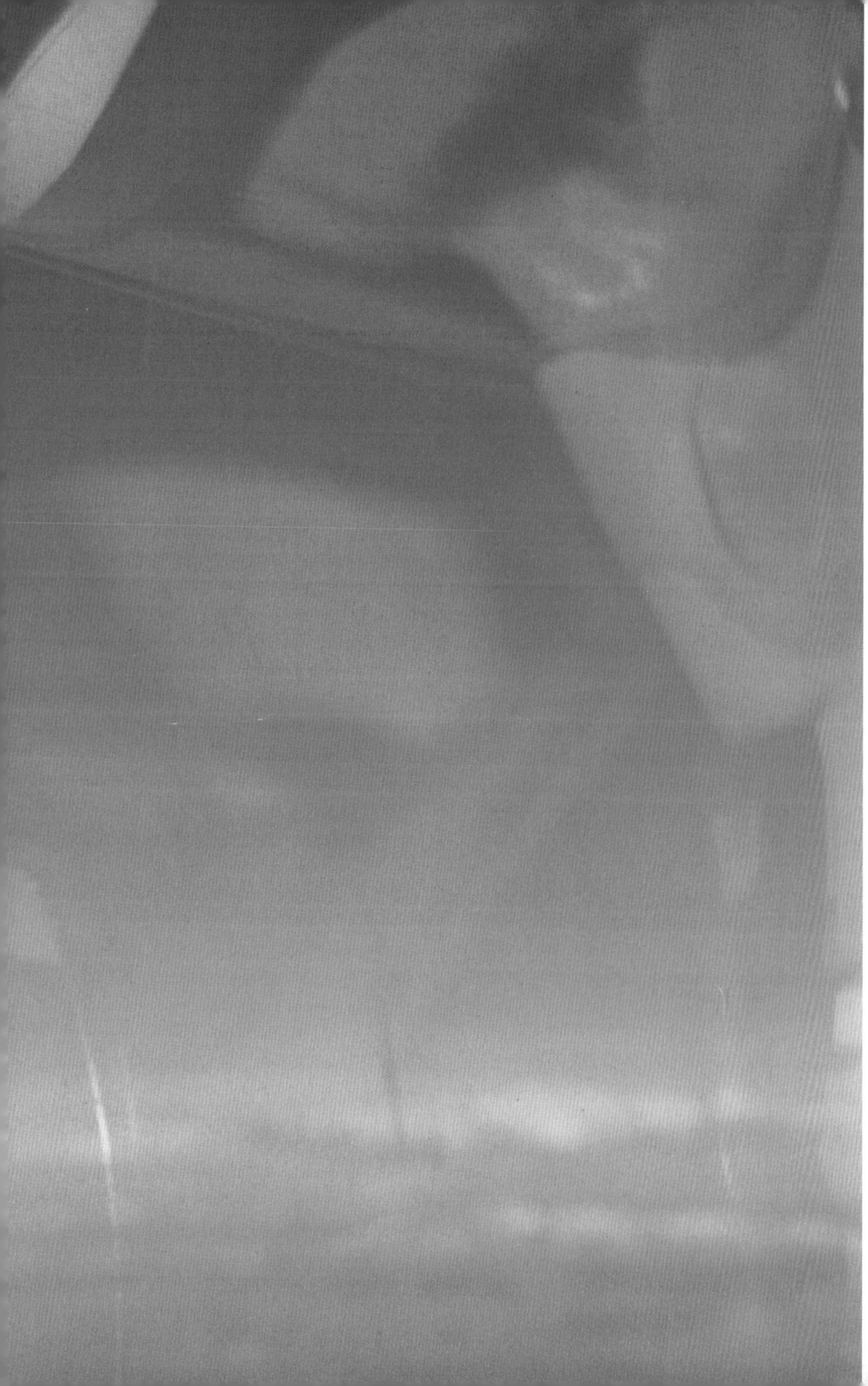

With eyes intently scanning the horizon, focused on infinity, TOPGUN adversary pilot and instructor Lieutenant-Commander Rinehart 'Rhino' Wilke maintains a lookout for the 'good guys', the visiting student fleet pilots. One of the most experienced pilots the Navy possesses, Rhino has spent many years flying fighters, both off carriers and as a much-valued instructor at TOPGUN.

A further downside in the move from Miramar to Fallon is the proximity to the desert and an awful lot of sand. When the wind gets up it can transport clouds of the abrasive silicon granules, depositing them liberally en route. Following such a sandstorm, the jets are treated to a thorough washing down. Designed for use on aircraft-carrier, where space is at a premium (even on the larger USN variety), folding wings are de rigueur, as demonstrated by this NSAWC Hornet.

Another successful mission performed, two TOPGUN adversary instructor pilots stroll in for a welcome coffee prior to debrief – part of which will involve viewing the Head Up Display (HUD) video tapes they both carry. Because of the dangerous nature of operating jets from aircraft-carriers, US Navy pilots are required to wear more survival equipment than just about anybody else. Equally as hostile as the Atlantic Ocean – but for different reasons – the vast, sun-scorched, rocky plains of the Nevada Desert are friend to no man. Should they have to eject, such survival kit would be equally welcome here.

The General Dynamics F-111 went into service with the USAF in 1967 and, employed as a bomber, has seen combat use in Vietnam, the US attack on Libya in 1986 and the Gulf War. The Aardvark was the first aircraft to successfully utilize Variable Geometry (VG) swing wings. Like the later F-14 and Tornado fighters, the F-111's wings can be swept forwards for more lift at slower speeds or aft at higher speeds.

A pair of F-111E 'Aardvarks' from the 79th Tactical Fighter Squadron at Upper Heyford in England close in on a KC-135 tanker, while a 74 Squadron Phantom holds off. This is the view awarded the boom operator who, using a flight control and the wings on the boom, 'flies' the refuelling arm to mate with the fighter.

Currently replacing the F-111 is the new, all-weather interdictor/strike variant of the F-15 Eagle, the Strike Eagle. The dedicated two-seat F-15E fighter bomber is a high-tech adaptation of the original single-seat air superiority Eagle and is one of the most potent and capable strike-fighters in the world today. The jets seen here are the flagships from the 492nd and 494th Fighter Squadrons belonging to the 48th Fighter Wing at Lakenheath in Suffolk, England.

LN
LN
492 FS

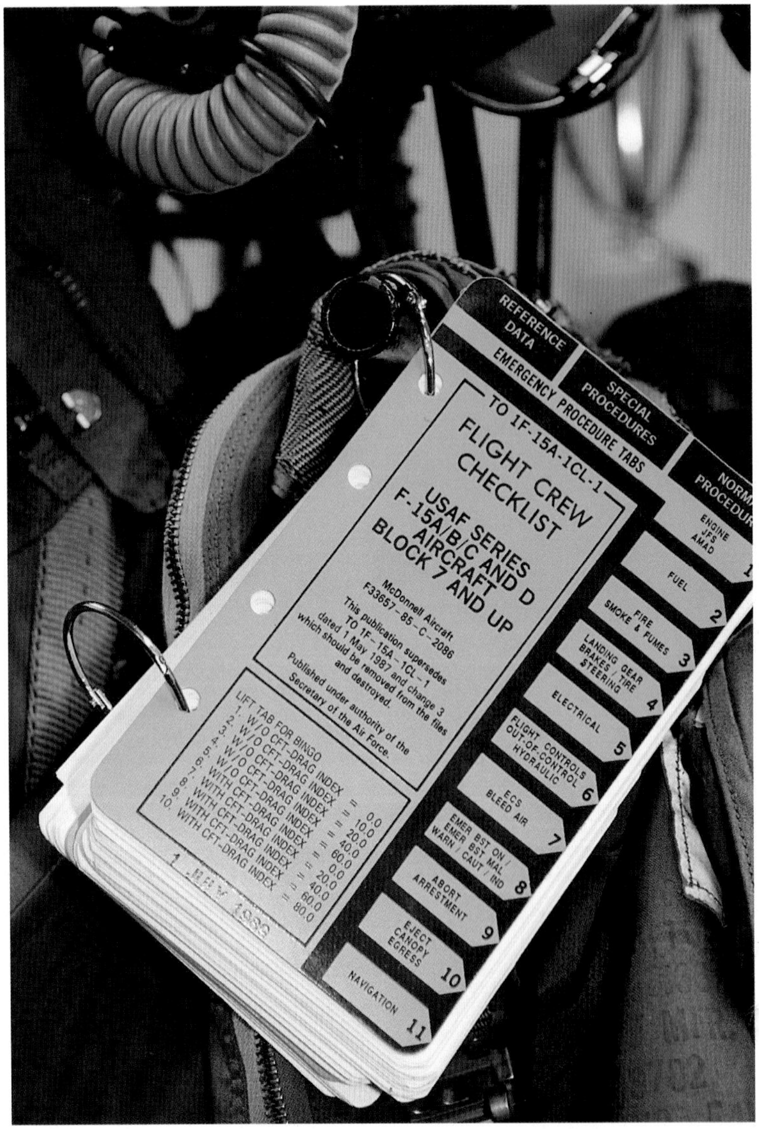

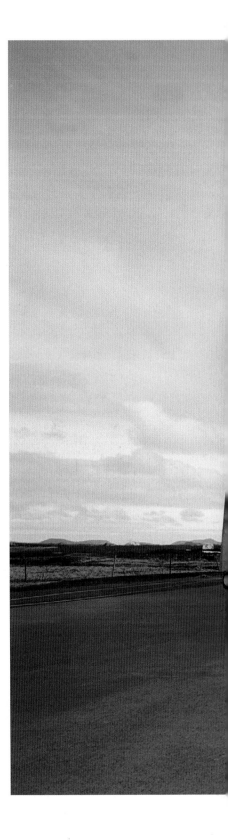

Captain Chuck 'Slapper' Wanebo of the 57th Fighter Interceptor Squadron based at Keflavik, Iceland, climbs aboard his awesome fighting machine, the F-15C Eagle. During the Cold War period, Iceland's strategically beneficial location in the North Atlantic deemed it prudent to deploy a fully dedicated air superiority fighter squadron there. For twenty-four hours a day, 365 days a year, the 57th FIS 'Black Knights' kept at least two jets on permanent alert status, ready to launch at a moment's notice to intercept any unidentified aircraft, the majority of which were Soviet.

14

Amid the haze of an unusually hot and sunny day in Iceland, having performed the last chance checks, a ground crewman removes the chocks from the wheels of a Black Knights F-15C as, in the background, two further jets await similar treatment. The Iceland Eagles were fitted with conformal fuel tanks, dramatically increasing the jet's endurance – a reassuring measure when taking into account the country's remote location. The tanks, fitted as standard on the F-15E Strike Eagle, give the jet a rather chubby appearance when viewed from the front.

Lieutenant-Colonel Paco Geisler, Director of Operations and F-15 Eagle driver of awesome experience, poses in full flight gear. Fastened about Paco's waist and legs is his anti-g suit. Plugged into the jet's pneumatic system, when under high force of gravity loading, compressed air is fed into bladders in the suit which expand, clamping forcefully around the pilot's waist and legs, helping to prevent blood from being forced down during high g manoeuvres, the result of which can lead to loss of consciousness.

Perhaps this weather is more what one would expect in Iceland as the 57th FIS flagship jet prepares to zoom off into the murk. Few people would even consider launching on a day such as this, but, for a Black Knights alert bird, it's all in a day's work.

A view through an Eagle's Head Up Display (HUD) as it taxis out in company with another F-15 and a pair of visiting Norwegian F-16s.

Reefing into the vertical, a brace of 57th FIS Eagles make the most of the superb weather at 25,000 feet and of the 34,000lbs of thrust to hand. Although now a relatively old aircraft – the first F-15 flew operationally back in 1975 – it is still an awesome fighter, quite capable of holding its own with most current generation jets, particularly at altitude. It was the principle air superiority fighter employed by the United States during the Gulf War, destroying thirty-four Iraqi aircraft in a twenty-five day period.

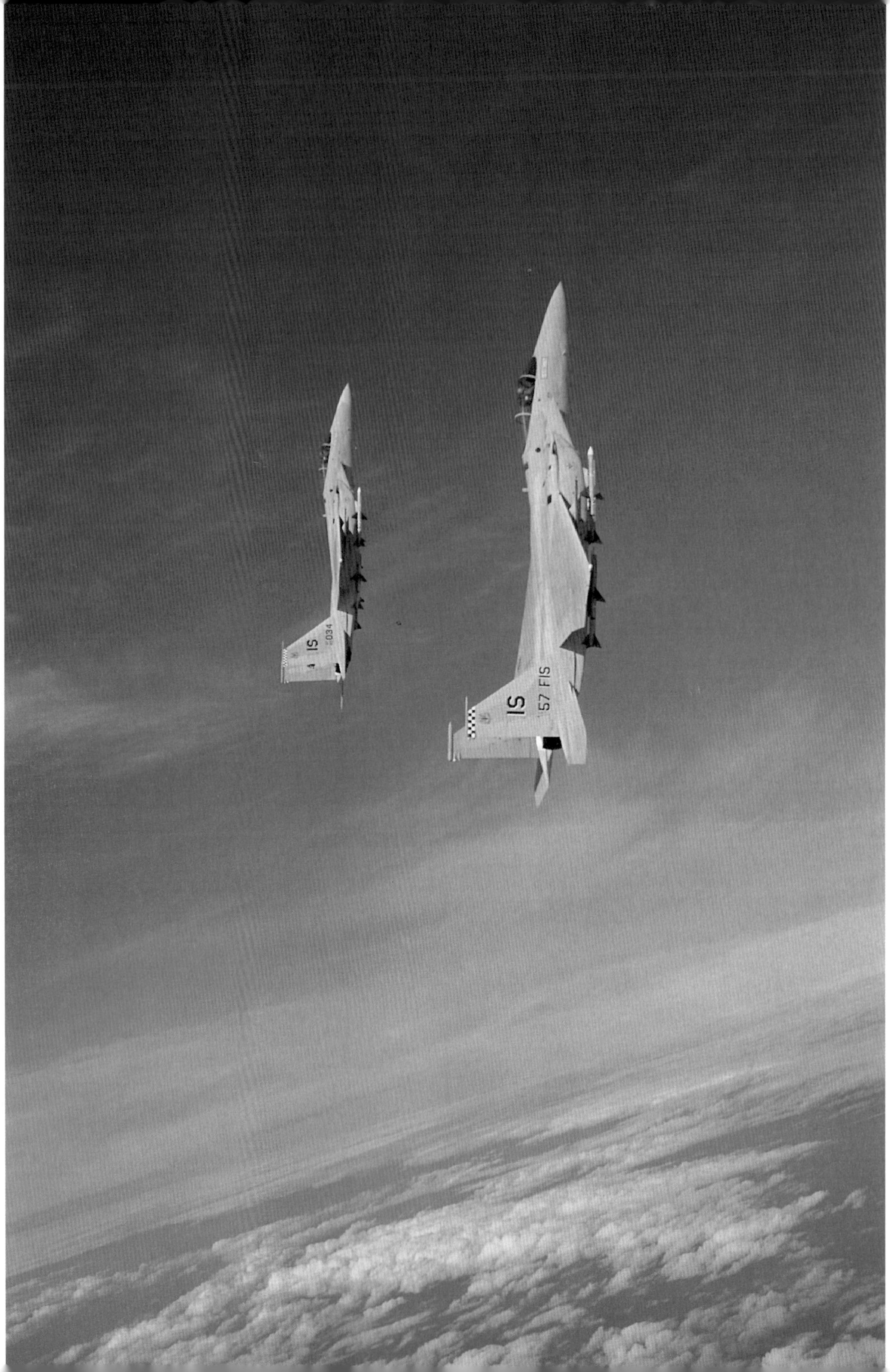

Every week a KC-135 tanker would deploy from the 100th Air Refuelling Wing at Mildenhall, England, to Temporary Duty (TDY) at Keflavik. These would be used to air refuel the 57th FIS jets to extend their airborne duration.

A cockpit eye's view from the back seat as Lieutenant-Colonel Al 'Disco' Peck plugs the F-15D into the KC-135 tanker. The black void forward of the boom on the underside of the tanker's fuselage is the operator's window, from which vantage point, on a different occasion, the picture on page 90 was taken.

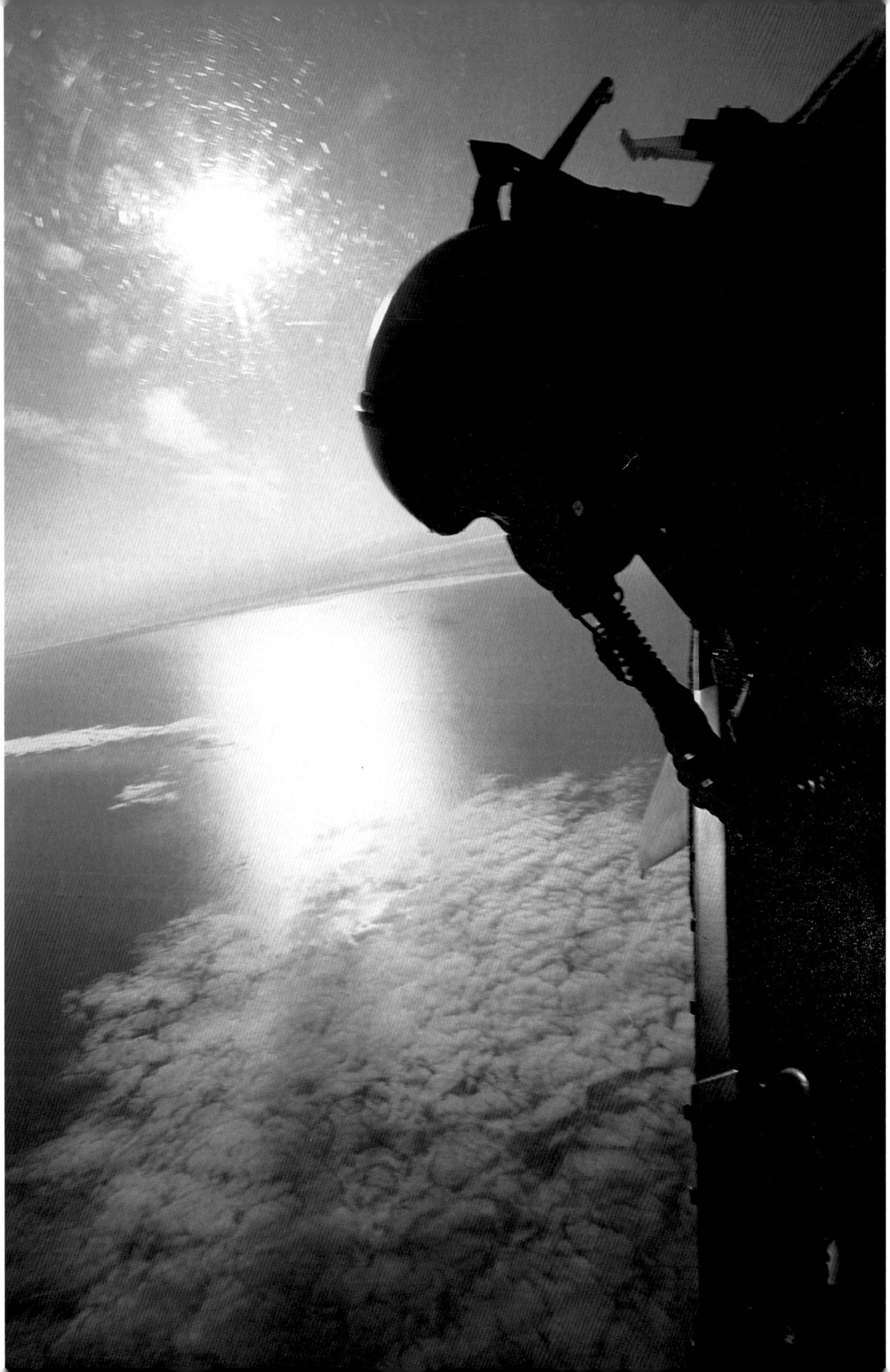

With the new found friendship between East and West, and the consequent defence cuts, many of the NATO bases located in Europe have now closed, including that at Keflavik, the protective F-15 shield above Iceland deemed surplus to requirements.

ULMER
FRANCE

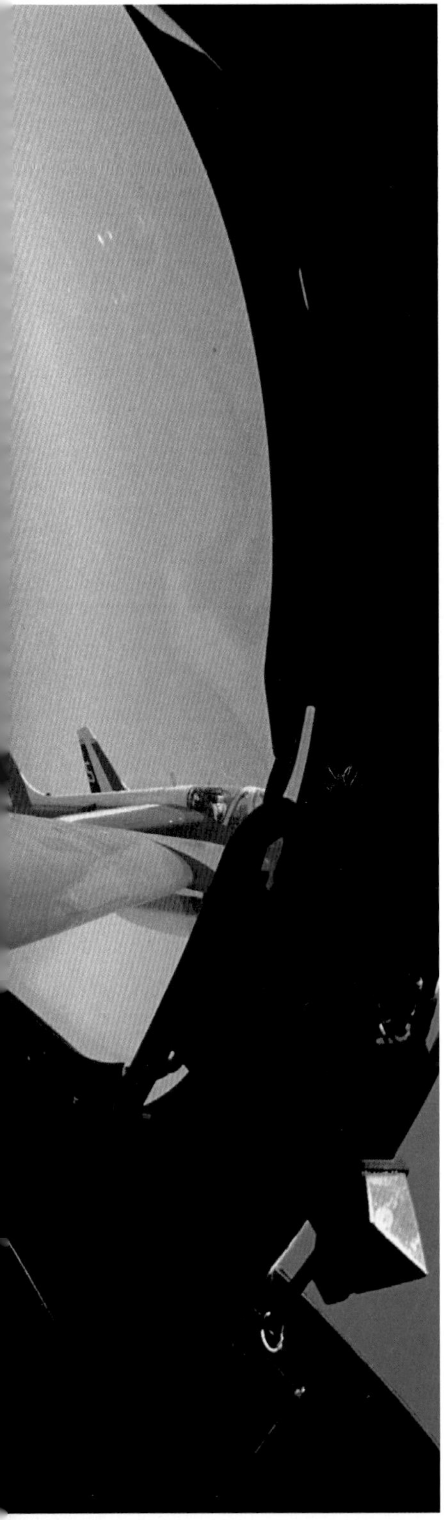

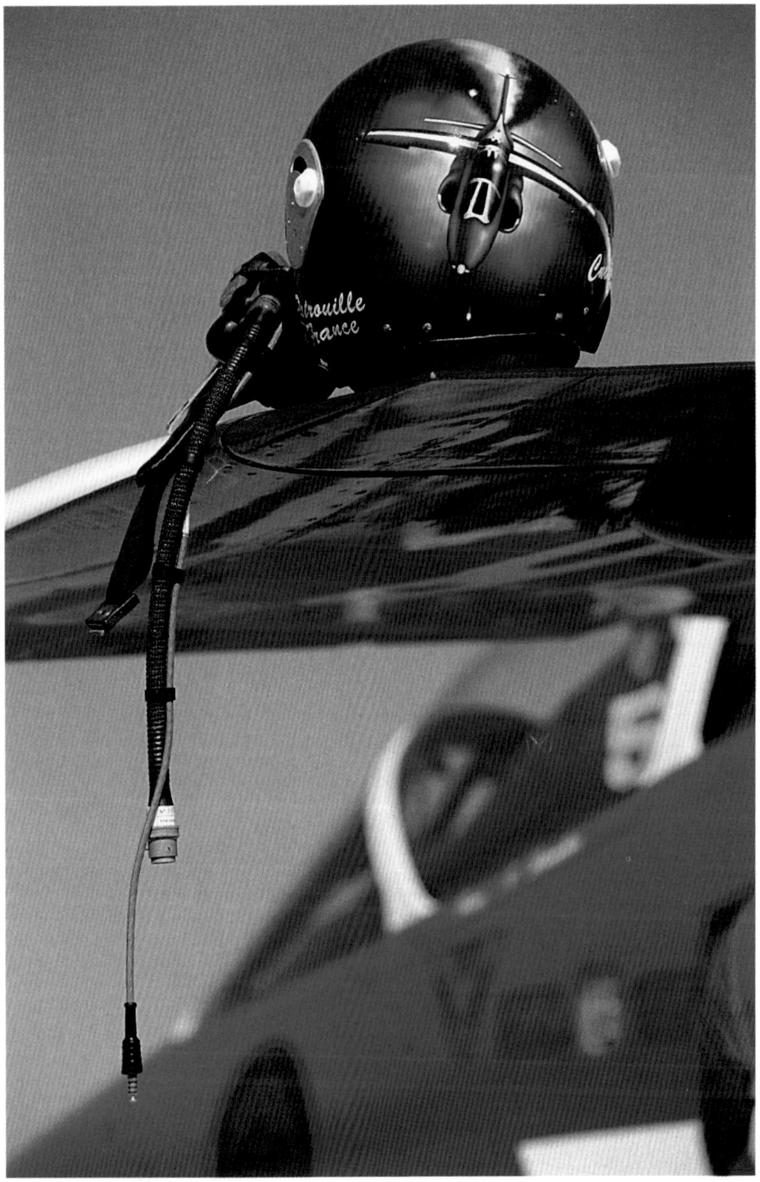

Above the Patrouille de France's home base of Salon-de-Provence, near Marseilles, the Team perform a perfect formation barrel roll during one of their pre-season training flights. We're riding in the cockpit of 'Athos 1', the Leader's jet, with Major Vincent Cousin. The formatting aircraft will follow Vincent faithfully through the manoeuvres, relying on his skill to fly smoothly, precisely and exactly to time.

Captain Philippe Morales prepares to taxi for Salon's runway. In the Patrouille de France (PAF) the Leader leads for just one year and, for the '98 season, thirty-year-old Captain Morales, currently flying in the 'Slot' position, will inherit the prestigious 'Athos 1' name tag.

On a hazy but hot and balmy day in April 1997, the PAF's eight-ship formation departs the Salon runway in two flights of four. The Patrouille first operated out of Salon-de-Provence, home of the 'Ecole de l'air' (French Air Force Academy), in 1964, the generally favourable weather conditions in this region of southern France being particularly appropriate for the Team's hectic winter training programme.

A view from Captain Nicolas Dauber's (alias Athos 5's) cockpit as the Patrouille de France formation peels off. Moments later it would be impossible to take pictures as Nicolas snaps the nimble Alphajet to the left in trail. The Patrouille first flew as such in 1953, and can therefore claim to be one of the oldest national aerobatic teams of all. Their current generation displays using the Alphajet advanced trainer, are flawless and, in partnership with such teams as the Red Arrows, Frecci Tricolori and the Blue Angels, the PAF are among the very best and most professional in the world.

Once again riding with Athos 5 (second left wingman), the eight perfectly synchronized PAF jets roll in Diamond formation.

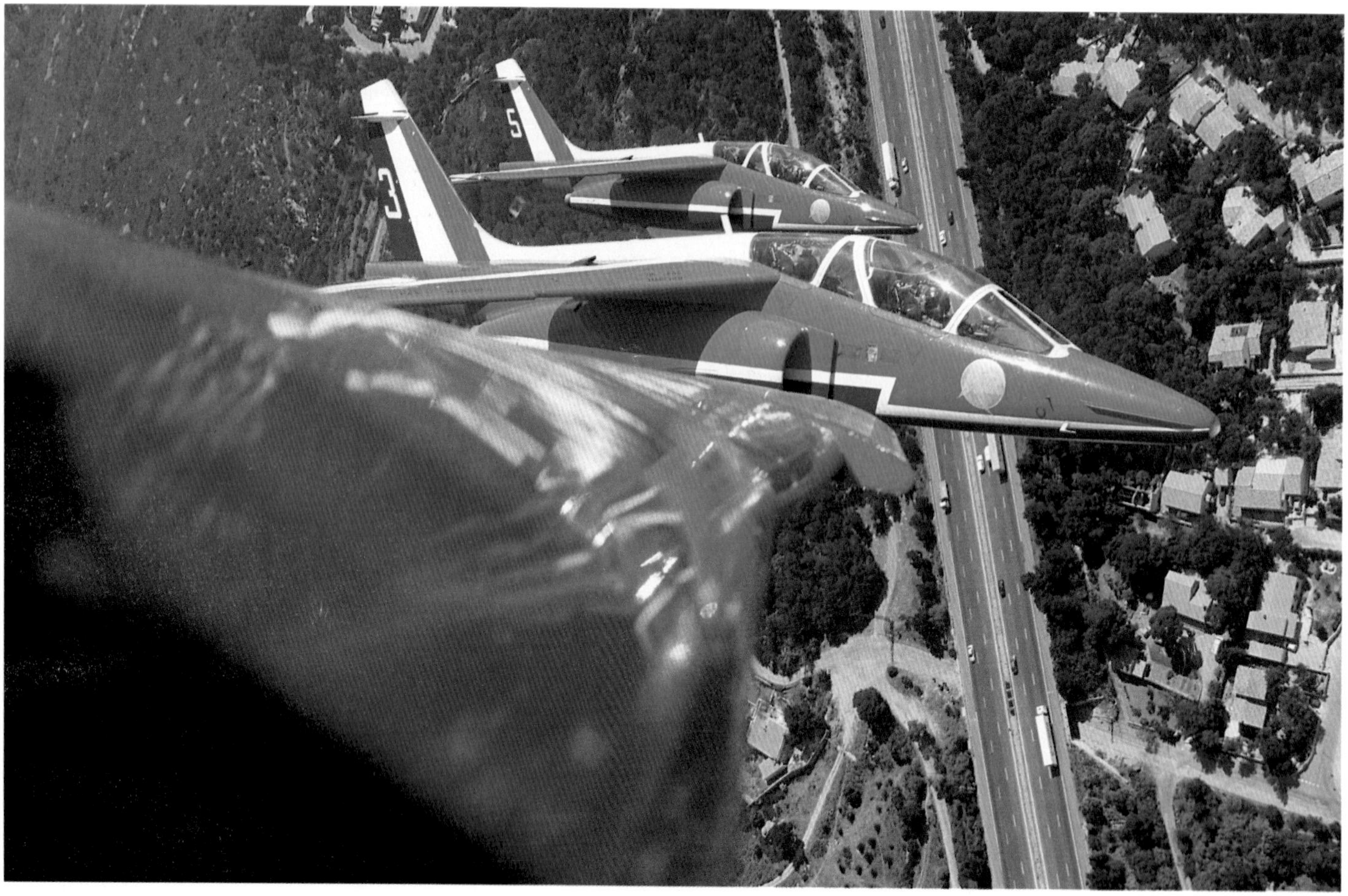

Rolling Diamond formation again, but this time an opposite viewpoint as we ride in the Leader's cockpit with Major Vincent Cousin, looking down, along the Alphajet's wing to Athos 3 and 5 – Captains Bertrand Boillot and Nicolas Dauber. Below us life goes on as usual, commuting traffic travelling along the main A7 motorway, largely oblivious to the human endeavour and spectacle unfolding in the skies above.

One of the Team's ground crew pays meticulous attention to detail as, having serviced the Alphajet's braking system, he prepares to securely wire lock the components in place. In the world of military aviation there exists a bond of mutual trust between the ground crews who maintain the aircraft and the pilots who fly them. Nowhere does such a bond exist more strongly than in the national formation aerobatic teams where often the pilots do not have the time to perform a 'walk around', instead relying implicitly on the care and professionalism of their ground crews.

ARMEE
DE L'AIR

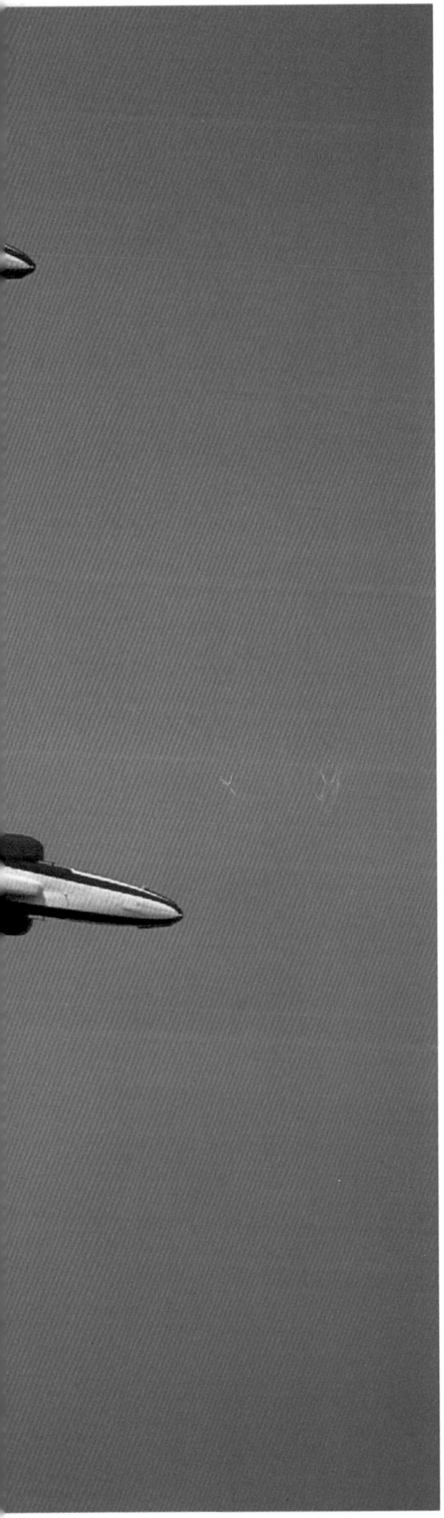

The precision of the leading jet formation teams is amazing, but it's only when one is privileged to actually fly with them during a full display that one can fully appreciate the skill, expertise and levels of concentration involved.

In common with all the other leading teams, each and every display that the Patrouille perform – be they pre-season training or in-season displays – is recorded on videotape for meticulous analysis and scrutiny. Whenever possible this is done at PAF HQ, as here, but often, when on the road during the display season, a hotel room has to suffice.

A No 1 Squadron pilot climbs aboard his Harrier in preparation for a training sortie on a decidedly damp and murky day at RAF Wittering. Military air crew accept the fact that their job entails flying in the most adverse conditions, should the situation demand.

In the hover with the sun immediately behind, this No 1 Squadron Harrier GR7 takes on a rather sinister, bat-like appearance. The spindly pair of outrigger wheels take little of the jet's weight, the Harrier's bulk being accepted by two sets of main wheels on the centre line beneath the fuselage.

Always a crowd favourite at air shows because of its undeniable, noisy presence in the hover, the amazing vertical or short take-off and landing (VSTOL) Harrier has seen extensive and very successful service with both the Royal Air Force and the US Marine Corps over the past twenty-five years.

The abnormally bulbous canopy of this Harrier identifies it as a T10 two-seat conversion trainer operated by No 20 (Reserve) Squadron. The downward angled thrust generated by the jet's single Rolls-Royce Pegasus engine vapourizes moisture on Wittering's tarmac runway as the Harrier completes its short take-off run.

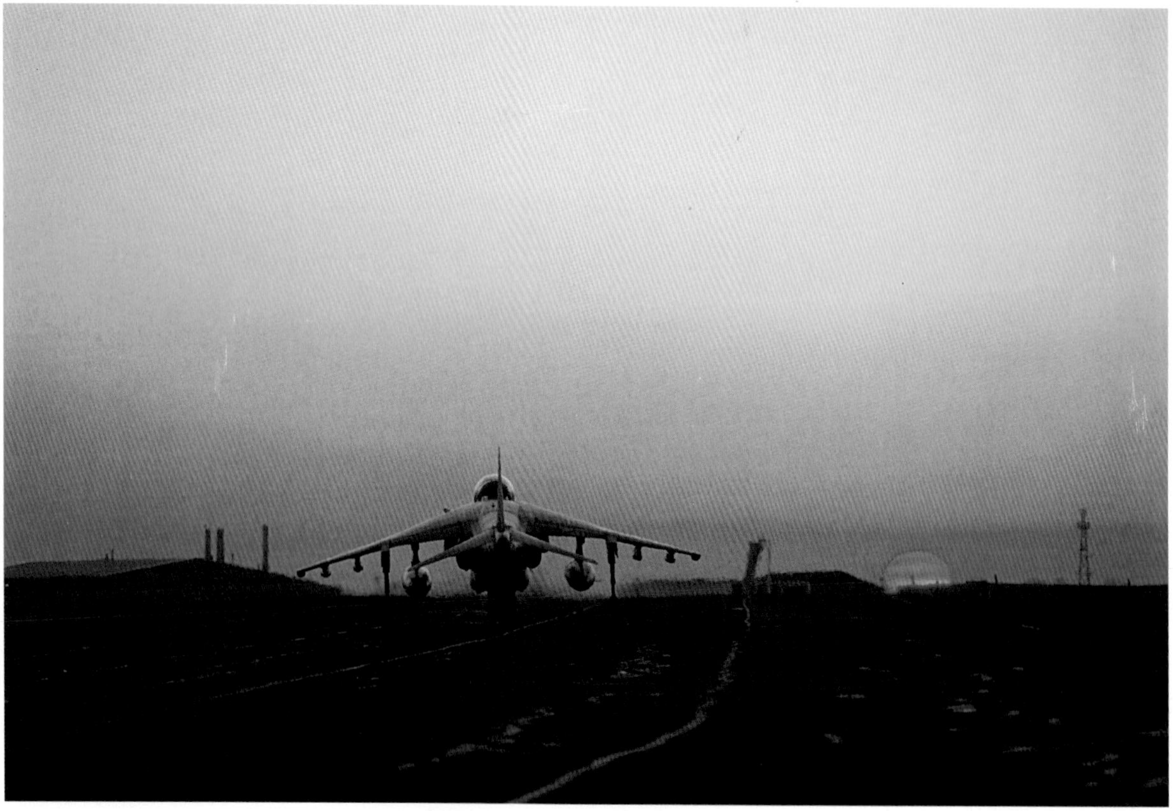